FROM ANGUISH TO HOPE

JODY SCHLOSS

To order additional copies of this book, contact:
Xlibris
844-714-8691
www.Xlibris.com
Orders@Xlibris.com

ISBN: Softcover   978-1-6641-4866-6
       EBook   978-1-6641-4395-1

Print information available on the last page

Rev. date: 01/20/2021

FOREWORD

I first met Jody in 1987 in Toronto when we were 14 years old. I had just emigrated from South Africa with my family. We met at a riding stable, where Jody kept her horse, and we became fast friends.

Our teenage years took us in many different directions, until we met again in Vancouver at the University of British Columbia after Jody returned from Cambridge University in England. Our friendship has endured more than 33 years so far.

After her accident, we were all very shocked and devastated while we waited for any sign that Jody would wake from her coma. Her mom, Gail, refused to give up and in true Jody form she proved the doctors wrong. Recovery was a long road for her, yet we started to see a drive and tenacity from Jody that began guiding her healing and her comeback. She never took "No" for an answer from anyone or any situation, instead finding a way to do whatever she set her mind to. I started admiring the way she persisted to attempt and re-attempt whatever she wanted to until she succeeded with her signature brave yet very kind spirit. She skied, sailed on the ocean, travelled to Thailand and South Africa, continued to ride horses - there was nothing and I mean nothing that deterred Jody in any way.

One of my favourite stories that I always remember occurred on a trip to South Africa. Jody was determined to go Bungee Jumping off a bridge and I was absolutely petrified and not willing to go. I was totally relieved when she decided that maybe it wasn't a great idea. Nonetheless, she did a Safari in a Game Park, went Micro lighting in Durban, danced the night away in Sun City, shopped at markets and sailed. There simply is no hurdle too big for Jody and there is nothing she won't try.

To further her Equestrian career, we attended 2010 World Equestrian Games together and it was during a dressage competition that Jody decided to ride for Canada. In 2012, with hard work and dedication, and a new horse named Inspector Rebus, Jody represented Canada in the London Paralympics. Jody's schedule was rigorous, she rode daily and worked out while still doing her daily tasks. Jody chose to do everything herself and it was her attitude and determination to succeed that inspires so many people around the world.

Jody has continued to reset her goals, dreams and aspirations for as long as I have known her and continues to defy what other people see as limitations. For Jody, that would simply be another challenge she will overcome, one way or the other. Jody flew out to my wedding in Vancouver 2015 and danced and celebrated with me, my family and friends. Yet again, I saw how nothing can stop Jody to pay tribute to our friendship.

You are holding in your hands another goal Jody set for herself to write a book. She did it. She wrote a book!

This book is not just an achievement and another goal achieved by Jody. It is a testament to Jody's character, persistence and her belief that you can do anything you want to in your life. Nothing can stop you if you have faith and belief in yourself. She is the true definition of a fighter and a go-getter.

Her fascinating story written with both poetry and prose will draw you in to the life of a remarkable person.
Her story will challenge you to rethink and recalibrate what could be possible for your life.
You are in for a treat with this book.
You may be moved more than you are ready for.
Embrace it, as Jody embraces her life every day.
Jody, you remain my inspiration and my very dear friend.
You have proved nothing is impossible.

Vanessa Kursan
Vancouver, Canada
2020

Vanessa & Jody, 2004
South Africa

DEDICATION

For my mother, Gail, who always believed in me.

CONTENTS

I AM

I am determined not to have limitations set upon me
just because I am different
I wonder if I will achieve my goals
I hear applause every time I do something I was never supposed to accomplish
I see myself with all my hard work delivering the desired ending
I want the desired ending
being able to walk and talk without difficulty
people seeing me as a person first, not a brain injury
I am determined not to have limitations set upon me
just because I am different

I pretend that I was not injured, and am still the person I was
I feel like a stronger person now
I touch what I want to achieve
I worry that the limitations will come true
I cry when I am seen as a brain injury, not unique
I am determined not to have limitations set upon me
just because I am different

I understand that I will never be the same as I was before
I say that my hard work will deliver the desired ending
I dream that I fly everywhere I want to go
I try to do the best I can at everything I want to accomplish
I hope that my wish will come true
I am determined not to have limitations set upon me
just because I am different

*The first two chapters of the book are co-written by Jody and Ariella. In
the rest of the chapters, Jody tells her story in her own voice.*

CHAPTER 1:

THE STORY BEHIND THE STORY

The story of Jody and Ariella working and writing together

The story began when Jody asked Ariella, a narrative researcher, to help her write her life story. Ariella does not have a title in Jody's life, nor a specific role. She helps her to think about herself as a person, not as a brain injury, to tell her story from her perspective, not a perspective she is supposed to have. She helps Jody be true to herself. At times Jody feels that her life is not hers anymore. She is expected to feel and behave in a certain way. Her way is not considered acceptable. In her book Jody wishes to point out the misconceptions people have about her and others with brain injuries.

Jody sees Ariella as a vehicle through which she can tell her story. As a vehicle, Ariella is "nobody." Yet she is somebody. A friend, a teacher, an intellectual, a somebody. Ariella is drawn to Jody's stories perhaps because as an individual she too has been silenced in one form or another in life, been dehumanized. They share an interest in stories, teaching, children, love, and relationships. At times when Ariella listens to Jody's stories, they cry. Tears well up in Ariella's eyes, and Jody can tell she feels deeply moved. Ariella responds with emotion, mind, body and soul. She listens more than she talks.

To tell Jody's story, Ariella gathered Jody's poetry, prose, and snippets of their conversations, contextualized these fragments, placed them in position, joined them together and represented them in this book for the reader.

They struggled with how to tell a multi-layered, multi-voiced story, bearing in mind constantly that it must have educational significance for others. They asked themselves what portrait they should paint of Jody for the reader. They wished to maintain Jody's dignity on her journey to recovery of self. They did not wish to sensationalize. They tried to present Jody to promote empathy and connection. They wanted to evoke in order to promote action and response, not pity. They did not want readers to turn away and say, "Thank goodness that's not me."

And so many questions arose. How should they present Jody's story? What form should it take? Hers is an individual story. Is it risky to use her life to generalize about brain injury? They recognized the responsibilities of presenting it, responsibility to the facts. Words can be so tricky. With this book, Ariella and Jody take the risk of using words, sometimes the words of others. Carl Leggo's (2003) words embody Jody's journey.

> I will not live with regret. I do not want to be staked to the miss(ed) opportunity, ….
> I will move on with heart and hope. My present will not be lost because of my past.
> Autobiographical writing is heart and hope and health for living in the present. (p.25)

CHAPTER 2:

WHY WRITE?

At their first meeting, Jody asked Ariella what she does. Ariella explained that she loves to tell stories and to listen to others' stories. For her doctoral thesis written in narrative form, she told her own story as a daughter, student, teacher, wife, and mother, and found the process transformative. Apparently, the teacher and children with whom she worked on her research, also found the process beneficial. "Why?" Jody asked her. Ariella replied,

> "Narrative is essentially about understanding, creating and living our lives through stories. Through creating stories we give our lives meaning. Story telling or writing is a way we make ourselves intelligible to ourselves and to each other. We make sense out of the chaos. Some find that Narrative helps make sense out of trauma while creating hope for a life not defined by the effects of that trauma. Telling and writing helps us to externalize and define the problems as separate from ourselves – creating a distance. In this way, we can examine and perhaps resolve our problems.
>
> We write about a quest to grow. We question our relationships, personal values and life priorities, and perhaps, a new story about a self that is wiser through experience grows in the telling." (2004)

Ariella said she saw her role with Jody as creating conversations that might help her to share her experiences and stories, face the problems the stories tell, and create alternative stories, new possibilities for relationships and new futures. Writing might be a way of accepting pain, fear, uncertainty and strife, but also a way to find a place of safety, security and serenity.

In her memoir *Almost There*, Nuala O'Faulian (2003) captures the effects of writing a life story. She writes,

> Whatever can be said about the other alleged therapeutic effects of autobiographical writing, ... one works - tidying up your memory the way you'd tidy a cluttered room.... A memoir may always be retrospective, but the past is not where its action takes place.
>
> I grew a skin over my wounds first by finding words for them and then purging the words of their power - by making them utensils in a job, a task....Making use of things makes them ordinary; they're kicked into shape by the time you have them doing what you want. (p.52, 187)

Ariella says that life comes first, which can then be transformed into art. And then people begin to transform themselves, hopefully, ultimately into better human beings.

It was Ariella's turn to ask Jody questions. She asked Jody why she wanted to write her life story. Jody answered,

> "I want to write my life story, describe the person I was, the experience I went through, and the person I wish to become so that I might help others who have been through the same experience to motivate them to keep trying. I will describe a girl who had her life planned out only to have those plans destroyed in a second. I will write about her life before the accident, her goals, how easy it was for her to achieve everything she wanted, and how after her accident, her life changed dramatically. I will describe the challenges she faced, continues to face, and how she deals with them daily. I will write about her life-long love of travel, teaching, and outdoor sports such as horse-riding, sailing and skiing. And despite her difficulties, she became very proud of herself for all her hard work and accomplishments." (June, 2004)

For a story to be heard and read it needs a form. The form reflects the content, and the content must reflect the form. Jody thought about the form for a while, and said to Ariella, "I want to write everything that was and is significant in my life in poetry. Then all I have to do is write the everyday life in prose."

Why poetry? Jody has given many reasons, and Ariella has collected them over time. Jody says:

> "I was actually surprised by how much I learned about myself by writing poetry. I don't know if what I write is even poetry, but it is my thoughts, thoughts I don't even know I have. The thoughts I express are the ones that I have the most emotional feelings about and are the ones I am most confused about.

> Writing poetry helps to sort out my thoughts and emotions. It makes me think! Sometimes I am overwhelmed, stressed and in pain. Poetry really helps me to think about what I am going through and makes me think about my real problems. It lets me find an escape from feeling that I have no way out.

> That's why I sound down and reflective in them. Perhaps if I were constantly air headed and happy, I wouldn't have anything to write about.

> The weird thing is I sometimes dream in poetry.

> When I write, I can feel my anger going away. Rather than talking and becoming emotional, I write poems and send them out to people. They will see why I am angry, and if they don't it's their personality flaw, not mine. I feel better after I write.

> The one thing I am learning is that the poems are very personal, almost too personal." (2005)

In this poem Jody expresses how she feels about writing poetry

Poetry

Putting everything down in words
PERSPECTIVE
Clears your MIND
Helps find the right solution

Downsizes the issue
Forces thoughts about alternatives
Realization of what you have
Compared to OTHERS

Granted your life is more difficult
Compared to OTHERS
Hate it
When others feel sorry for you

Should be proud of your
MANY ACCOMPLISHMENTS
Despite all OBSTACLES
Focus on achievements

Write about them
It's not fair to compare yourself to those
In your old life that you long for
Stop, take time to realize how special your new life is

Those who read her poetry, respond strongly to it. Here are some of those reactions.

Her physiotherapist wrote:

> Jody,
> Your poems are brilliant lady!! You know this may be a new vocation for you!!
>
> Can I send them to the rest of the staff? Can we print them up on nice paper and put them in the office? You know there are no words that can express how proud I am of you. You are quite remarkable, and it is wonderful to participate in your journey, even though it is tragic. You have the capacity to change many things for brain injured people and the rest of us. Although you learn from your team, your team learns from you too. I admire your resolve and tenacity. Keep up all the good work but remember to stop and smell the roses from time to time. (October 2004)

Another therapist wrote:

Thanks so much for sending your poetry. It's quite amazing and gives a real window into what makes you tick. It will be good to talk with you more about it.

And another:

Thank you for sharing this with me. I found it very powerful, poignant and just unbelievable. You really get across the complexity of what is so automatic for most people. An amazing piece of poetry. (April, 2005)

One of her university professor's wrote:

Thank you very much for your poetry. I enjoyed all of it…You have a fine sense of sound and voice. Do keep writing poetry. (August, 2005)

Ariella helped Jody write about her life experiences in prose and poetry.

She began by introducing herself to her readers as she is today.

CHAPTER 3:

NEW BEGINNINGS

In this chapter, Jody speaks in her own voice.

Let me tell you a bit about myself, my disability, and how in one second a life can be changed forever. My name is Jody Schloss. I am 34 and single. I have a brain injury. On June 20th, 1996, my car rolled over because of a faulty design. I was driving with a friend to San Bernardino, CA. She died in the accident and I suffered a closed head injury. I hurt the back of my brain, the brain stem, not the front. The front of your brain controls your personality, cognitive functions, and intellectual capacity. The part of my brain that was harmed controls the physical aspects. I am not paralyzed but am in a wheelchair as my trunk or torso is very unstable, my muscle coordination is poor, and I have trouble moving my limbs safely and effectively. I also have a severe speech impediment called dysarthria.

At the time of the accident, no one could tell what part of my brain was hurt. It was clear that I was hurt, because I was in a coma. Originally all my vital signs were very unstable, indicating injury to the front of my brain. However, it soon became obvious I hurt my cerebellum. Damage to different parts of the cerebellum or control units results in a variety of movement disorders. These include:

1) problems coordinating voluntary movements
2) trouble controlling timing and force of the movement
3) movements may be wavering and jerky when trying to pick up an object.

This jerkiness is called cerebellar ataxia. In both speech and movement, damage to the cerebellum takes away the auto-pilot switch. So now I have to think about everything I do. Speech and movement are very complicated, as are most everyday activities. For example, I used to walk home with a friend from school and talk on the way. Today this is too complicated to manage. Now even in my chair I have to stop if I'm going to talk, so I can focus all my attention on my speech. This one small area of my brain plays a large role in the production of language as well as movement. Although I did hurt my brain, I do not have any symptoms of Aphasia, a common result of brain damage. Aphasia often includes the inability to find and produce the appropriate word, comprehension, and remembering simple English grammar and spelling. What I have is a motor speech disorder. For both speech and movement, I think I am telling my body to do one thing, but my brain intervenes and confuses it. This is referred to as Ataxia.

I will try to relate Ataxia to linguistics and speech. Whoever made up the English language made speech and linguistics the two hardest words to say! In phonology we learn that we do not understand how we make a word but have to say it in order to hear and understand how we say it. I do not have that advantage. Nothing for me is automatic anymore.

My speech pathologist comes weekly to help me understand how to make speech. This has been a very long learning process, especially since my soft palate or velum is paralyzed. I wear a tool called a palate lift in my mouth. It does not cover the entire gap like your soft palate does, or I would not be able to make the nasal sounds or breathe out of my nose. This makes it difficult to understand me at times, because the air still escapes through my nose making all my oral consonants sound less crisp and distinct.

My palate lift consists of a piece of metal like a retainer with a long pink appendage which covers part of the gap. The back of my tongue is also paralyzed, making the velar sound's "k", "g", and "ng" next to impossible for me to say.

Before I say anything, I also have to think about whether a sound is voiced or voiceless. I also have to think about place of articulation. For example, it is hard for me to make the beginning sound of my name…"J". My speech pathologist told me to say the voiceless "sh" sound and add voice. Now sometimes I can say the "d" sound before that, making the affricate.

With my palate lift, voiceless sounds are a lot easier to say. There is a lot less thinking involved. This is why it is easier for me to say the affricate "ts" than the affricate "dz".

Respiration is also difficult for me. I have been through a lot of breathing training.
Ataxic Dysarthria is defined as follows:

RANK	Speech Production Errors
1	Imprecise consonants
2	Excess and equal stress
3	Irregular articulatory breakdown
4	Distorted vowels
5	Harsh voice quality
6	Prolonged phonemes
7	Prolonged intervals
8	Monopitch
9	Monoloudness
10	Slow rate

I have all of these traits to some extent. I have monoloudness, but due to the air that escapes, my speech is very quiet. I have what is labeled as severe dysarthria. This means that I have these traits fairly severely. However, I am aware that there are some in a worse situation than I am in.

People say it is a milestone that I am now able to make the tragedy about me and not about the consequences it had for others. It is a milestone because I am now willing to accept that my life will never be the same. This was a very hard sentence for me to write, so I may not be at that point yet. The one thing I can definitely say is this has been a long and hard journey. People say that there is one specific event in their life that has taught them more about themselves than any other. My event was more life altering than usual. I was lucky that, despite its disastrous consequences, I learned about how strong I really am. On the first anniversary of my accident, my neuro-psychologist made me go out and buy myself a birthday cupcake to celebrate the beginning of my new life. I did not necessarily want a new life, but that's what I was given. I had the choice of being disappointed and living in the past or celebrating my new beginning. I would be lying if I said I was happy living my new life in place of my old life. However, I decided that the only way I would enjoy my life was if I worked hard to make it what I wanted it to be.

In 2004, I moved out of a 24-hour supervised living apartment for the head injured into my own apartment. One day I decided to take a walk on my own in the gardens of my apartment building. I have a mouth-piece that helps me talk, and also use a talking computer to make my speech clear however, on this particular day, I did not take the talking computer with me. In the poem I wrote below, I share with you, the reader, a dream I had the night before exams. The poem reveals my anxiety, but also what it takes for me to perform daily activities such as walking and talking.

Explosion

walking up to my building
greeting someone,
telling my name
No problem, right?

Walking -
what's involved?
pelvis straight
trunk directly over top
legs directly underneath pelvis
hips even, not jutting out to side
All elements in place,
Or
you fall!
Sucks to be you!

Talking -
what' involved?
introduce myself
"Hi, my name is Jody Schloss."
"h" is silent
requires air to make the breathing out sound
"i" like the "y" in "my" requires two movements
the "aa" sound at the beginning is open
then a smile for the "ee" sound
my is easy because the "m" is nasal.
so just say it
the "y" requires two movements
"n" and "m" are nasal, another easy word

the "s" sound in hard to say
it gets harder
"s" is silent, depends on vibration with the tongue up
"J" is like a "sh" sound with voice
"o" and "y" are vowels
so easy
just make the shape with your mouth and use voice
"d" is like the silent "t" only with voice
tricky to have everything in place
"Schloss" is a joke it's so hard
start with the silent "sh" sound
then "lo" which is easy
then "ss" sound which is harder at the end of a word
Trying to combine both is next to impossible
They are not automatic anymore
require a lot of brain power

Invited to go for a walk in front of apartment building
think: can handle it,
won't go far
go to front of building in wheelchair
get up:
Remember
everything must be in a straight line
legs directly over pelvis
reach the end of the walkway
without falling
turn around
see man approaching
walks up to me and introduces self
says he is the new superintendent
my turn
try to stop and lean against wall
but he keeps walking
Nervous!

I start, trying to
Remember
keep everything in line
move one crutch, then the opposite leg
in that order
or
will be seeing the ground much closer that I wish!
start to talk
get through "Hi, my name is…"
concentration difficulties, but manage

Now tough part,
Remember
keep everything in line when moving
to say "J" for m name
make a "sh" sound and use voice
"o" and "y" are easy,
know the movements
"d" requires movement of "t" with voice
concentrate
Remember
keep right hip in
not jutting out
pelvis over legs,
shoulders over legs

hard part: Schloss
make "sh" sound:
tongue up to roof of mouth
"get vibrations"
Remember
crutches go first then the leg
close call
tried to move both at once
continue with name,
"lo" is easy
have to get movements correct
now for the last "s" sound

start

Loud "Boom"

Superintendent asks tenant for help
gathering the blown up pieces of "Jody".
Put all the pieces back together
place on a bench outside on the walkway
dazed, frazzled, bewildered
"Jody" comes back to life
shaking her head in disbelief
tenant asks Jody, "what happened?"
Jody grabs her aching head in terror
More talking

Superintendent laughs
"Brain overload?"
Jody laughs, and nods her head

Despite many obstacles and difficulties, I graduated with a Bachelor of Arts from the University of British Columbia. Here is a poem I wrote describing what it was like to be a student with a brain injury, the graduation event, my feelings about becoming a graduate, and the struggles I face to enter graduate school, and fear of not finding employment in the future.

Graduation- from my perspective

I'm finally receiving that piece of paper
A degree that should have taken *four* years took me *fifteen*
I finished 5 years ago, but needed more courses to get into Education
Always feel like I have to make excuses

I can't make up for past mistakes
Before my accident University was about PARTYING and socializing
Never studied hard for those dreaded MARKS
Rather, spent time in a PANIC worrying about not focusing

After 5 years of school – ROLL-OVER
News of failing and remaining in second year
NOT A surprise!
Not depressed – had my goal to accomplish

Decided to keep goal of being a teacher
Wanted to teach the deaf. They wouldn't care if I couldn't speak!
New goal - to learn Sign Language
Started from the beginning. Very hard

Couldn't see, so took first course at Seneca with mom
Mom dropped out. Too hard to be translator, and also learn
Continued alone. Determined
Consulted Director of Deaf Education at UBC, very positive

OK – new goal set
I'm a harder worker now
Accident had an effect
But I can do it

PANIC ATTACKS over inability to write coherent essays
never learned how
caused extreme unpleasantness
FEAR OF FAILURE resulted in even more FAILURE

Spent HOURS taking notes from books
only to fail to combine them into an essay
Developed new attitude after accident
Unfortunately marks did not reflect my new attitude

Took psychology courses, still managed 95%
But needed English as a "teachable"
Essays became more conquerable
But still spent many hours and needed extensions

Even bought a little computer to take notes at library
went to the library three times a week for three hours at a time
So much stress and strain
For another degree - an English degree

Does a degree imply greater knowledge?
A way to improve yourself?
Seems like it's all about getting those letters to put after your name
That's not my goal

I know I want to work in Education
Children are the highlight of my life.
I have to make my graduation into a steppingstone
A celebration

Believing in myself and not letting my marks define me
was incredibly hard for someone who sought approval from others
everything I do must benefit me
not meet others' expectations

Knew I could do it, despite continually being told I couldn't
Gave me inner strength to prove everyone wrong
Goal set: finally achieved!
Onto next goal!

On the actual day, for the first time I felt excited!
First we found the gown and hood that I was to wear and I put it on
I was then given my hat and tassel
Next came my actual diploma!

It is only a bachelor's, but given my new challenges
it is an INCREDIBLE accomplishment!!
I was once very defensive about calling my accomplishment incredible!
Just because I couldn't walk or talk properly did not make me ABNORMAL!!
It made me BRAVE!!
When they called my name I was so EXCITED!!
They opened the door and I started walking
the chancellor came up to me, probably feeling sorry for me

said, "You don't have to walk the whole way unless you want."
Of course being me, I kept walking!

Perhaps he wanted to turn the fifteen-minute painfully slow walk for me
into the two-minute stroll it was for everyone else

I started on my long journey across the stage
lifting my knees up high exactly like I'm not supposed to, I was nervous!!
I stopped ever so often to ask where I should stop to have the professional picture taken
I never did find out, but apparently every time I paused the audience was egging me on!

As I neared the other side of the stage the clapping got louder
I was not sure if they were happy for me or just wanted me off the stage!
The clapping culminated in a standing ovation
Just before I walked off, I heard native drums beating in the background

Just holding a piece of paper that said I was finished made me giddy!
I was so happy and excited
It wasn't a BIG deal to most of my friends
to me it was a HUGE deal! Getting my actual degree
made me so PROUD!!!!!!!!!!!!!!!!!!!!!!

WOW! WHAT A GREAT FINALE!!!!!

A day of celebration certainly brought lots of confusion!
Actual event brought out many new feelings
Proud was not something I felt before that day
Embarrassed that it had taken me so long had been my emotion
A celebration for what I had been through was an unexpected surprise
I got the applause because I persevered
Truth was I grew as a person after my accident
I learned to change what I could, but to accept what I couldn't.

I learned many things from my accident
that horrible things can happen beyond your control
it is better to be happy with yourself
than be miserable just because you are not "Perfect"

"Perfect" according to whose standards?
what is the point of being so hard on myself?
hard lesson to learn!
Tragic near-death experience forced me to learn

Life is too short and precious
I grew up quickly after my accident
I learned to like myself for who I was, not what I was
Another hard lesson to learn

At my first class after graduation
It felt good to be in a class where everyone was PROUD of me
I learned about childhood suicide, how to deal with children
here's where I belong!

I knew what I wanted.
Pursued it until
THE LETTER arrived
Saw my life's mission vanishing in flames

have always wanted to be a teacher
stuffed animals were my students
can NOT be a teacher
What now?

UNTHINKABLE DILLEMA
Everyone goes through this after graduation
does NOT make it any easier
At least THEY have choices

Everything I have always wanted rests on my desire to work with children
Have to find someway to make it work
Will be an Educational Assistant, still working with kids that way
Will enroll in class to at least try to complete part of goal

Will work be available as an EA?
case manager made it quite clear; voice would limit my ability to teach
listen or ignore? Ignore!
Better to listen to people with knowledge of my capabilities

Going well. Lots of support from the school where I work
The TEACHERS feel there is a place for me
Say I will have more work than the average teacher
seems to be the story of my life! Is that what I really want??

But how do I fit Sign Language into the equation, make it an advantage?
So many disadvantages.
WHY CAN'T SOMEONE JUST TELL ME WHAT TO DO?

Would I listen if they did?
Probably not! Have to make up own mind.
Decision made or not? NOT Too many variables
Is working hard what I really want?
What I really want is to be HAPPY
Maybe become a teacher. Go to school for Education and have the option

Maybe be a tutor and help deaf young adults learn English
Maybe become a literacy instructor after all!
I simply want to be helpful
Helpful. How?

YES!!
I always learn from writing poetry
Now I have learned I want to pursue my dream!
So much advice about what path to take
I will follow my heart

Jody and her parents at her UBC graduation

Jody with her mom and brother Michael at her UBC graduation

I find it funny when I am asked to set realistic goals for myself for the next few years. It is funny because no one ever considers my goals and aspirations realistic, yet I still make them and usually accomplish them. As the number of years since my injury increase, my goals become much more complex, and not as easy to obtain. My goals are no longer drinking a liquid, or pushing my wheelchair down a hall on my own. I can only hope now that my goals are attainable and not merely fantasy.

Although I know that people like my therapists are not trying to limit me, I still have the drive to try to complete more than they feel is attainable. For example, my physiotherapist who is very supportive, feels that due to the slowness of my walking and my hectic lifestyle, I will most likely never be able to walk independently to all my activities. Her comments might be realistic, but I am not willing to give up. It still remains a goal I am determined to accomplish. Another goal that others do not feel is realistic is my goal of driving myself to all of my activities. Though my occupational therapist and physiotherapist supportively encourage me to strive towards this goal, I know they doubt I will accomplish it. I will limit myself to drive only where I absolutely have to go. I am going about it safely and using a computer program to complete the first stages. I will only continue if I am deemed safe to drive. I too am concerned for my safety and the safety of others.

Career wise, my goal has always been to help others and in particular, to work with the disabled. That was my goal even before my accident. After my accident, I decided that the deaf would not mind if I could not speak properly, so I would teach through Sign Language. Originally, I thought I might study towards my Master's in deaf education. I even had meetings at York, University of Alberta, and UBC about enrolling in Deaf Education. However, I was told that I cannot go into this profession because now with cochlear implants, the deaf are learning oral speech, not sign language. Teachers of the deaf must be able to teach speech. Also, the deaf are now mainstreamed in the schools which means I would have to go to many schools on one day. Not all schools are accessible. So I dropped this plan and decided to become an Educational Assistant so that I can work in one school with one child all day. I completed the Educational Assistant course at George Brown College in Toronto.

After my graduation with a BA in English and Psychology, I applied to UBC to begin a Bachelor of Education degree. To meet the requirements, I submitted evidence of a year's placement in a school for "normal" children, a neuropsychological report stating I was capable, and a report from my speech pathologist who came to observe my interaction at school. If I were admitted, I would continue on to do a Master's of Special Education. The admission department is not satisfied. In the meanwhile, I completed a year of an Educational Assistant course at George Brown College. I also had a placement at Bloorview (a school for the mentally and/or physically disabled), to determine if I am capable of taking on this position. If I decide that I am not capable, a new chapter of my life will begin, as I will be searching for new goals.

The process of applying for courses I am interested in is a painful and difficult one for me. Since my graduation I feel that a chapter in my life is closing, the chapter of school, particularly at the University of British Columbia where I studied towards my undergraduate degree and was happiest. I cannot pursue any of these dreams, so I feel lost. I realize that my goals and aspirations for my future may seem far-fetched, yet they remain the goals and aspirations I will strive for until completion.

Here is a poem I wrote in which I express my disappointment and sadness.

Missing

I should be happy.
A chapter of my life is finally closing
Why do I feel so lost and alone
This should be exciting

I am used to knowing my eventual goal
Part of my drive was from knowing
that eventually I will be out of here
somehow that took the pressure away from
having to be content with my life here

Everything will be different in Vancouver
It will be like the way it was before the roll-over
Part of me always wanted to believe that this
nightmare wasn't really happening

On a recent visit to Vancouver, I arrived at my old residence
and started CRYING
It should have been a very happy trip
BUT it was a reminder of what I no longer have

Even seeing my friends was a reminder that
EVERYONE has moved on
WHY do I still worship "COLLEGE DAYS?"
as a friend put it, definitely an AMERICAN

I am doing everything I can to get back to Vancouver
when there, I went to the Faculty of Education
to look for other options to
get to live in Vancouver again.

True it is beautiful, and has all the activities I love
like skiing, sailing, horseback riding and rock climbing
life is more than sports, and connections career wise
The real problem is I am lonely

Solution to problem:
make enjoyable life here, and try to improve life
So if move it will be due to the location
not seeking what I don't have here

EASY SOLUTION right?
WRONG!!!!
Why is this such a dilemma?

Shouldn't be searching for happiness

Need to be happy with life now, before searching for fulfillment
Think about it…even before University was content with life
Moved for experience, not for happiness
fell in love with the city

TIME changes everything
time to start living life and becoming happy NOW
So if I do move, it will be in search of ADVENTURE
NOT HAPPINESS

I have described myself to you, the reader. Now I will try to explain how I arrived at this place. I will begin at the beginning, my childhood, growing up in Edmonton, Alberta.

CHAPTER 4:

CHILDHOOD MEMORIES

My parents, brother and I were born in Edmonton. My parents divorced when I was 5. When I was 11, I moved to Toronto with my mother and brother. However, it remained a yearly tradition that on my birthday my parents would take me out to a Japanese Steakhouse together. My mom said that as a child I always wanted to do everything with them together. I always wanted a happy family. It's funny because I can remember all the times I was with both my parents. At my bat mitzvah, I sat between them and held both their hands. The settlement of my court case after my accident coincided with my birthday and again I asked both my parents to join me at a Japanese Steakhouse.

Ever since I was a child, I always wanted to be a teacher. When I was little I used to play 'teacher' with my stuffed animals and I used to force my brother be my student. I did not give him a choice about doing this. My dad even bought me a little chalkboard so I could pretend I was really teaching. I used to play school with my friends too. I wasn't a very forgiving teacher.

Here are two poems I wrote about my parents, grandparents and siblings.

FAMILY

Family
Always feeling loved
Knowing that I will always be considered
SPECIAL

Family
Split apart
Mother
Never says anything negative
To turn children against father
Fun and creative

Motto:
Keep children busy
Doing activities they enjoy
Ensure pride in accomplishments
Children's ignorance about the difficulty of this job

Help with school work
Do everything to make sure
That children are helped with every
NEED

Father
Always makes children feel special
Spoiled rotten
When young ride on his legs
Good morning treat

Help children achieve their goals
Buys chalkboard for daughter who
Teaches stuffed animals important
Elementary school math

Special trips taken
To explore and find adventure
Teaches children to strive
To achieve their goal

Younger brother
Only one year and a half younger
More like a best friend

Play together
Dress stuffed animals in tinfoil outfits
Mom: bathing kids together is a good idea!
Mom, she's grabbing me again
Why don't I have one?
Bratty sister

Brother
Quiet through sister's difficult
TEENAGE YEARS
Never helping brother with any
Of his issues

Sheva
Black and white furry loveable creature
SUPER LICKER
UNCONDITIONAL LOVE
Won't sleep with you
Not sleepy
Don't need pillow

Mother's parents
Like second parents
There to help mother
Through tough times

Loving
Teach importance of family
Unconditional love
Want to make them proud

Grandma
Cooks delicious food
Prauchas and plum cake
Teaches granddaughter to knit and rug hook
While relaxing or watching TV

Grandpa
Takes walks with children
In Scottsdale, Arizona
Takes on his cart at work
Always makes yummy breakfasts
After sleepovers

Teaches children about the importance
Of their religion
Religion becomes family centered
IMPORTANT

Father's parents
Loving
Visits out to Camrose
In grade two: Alone
Very grown up

Playing at the pool in Palm Springs
Going in the hot tub with grandpa
While he does his exercises

Grandma
Always knows what to wear
Playing hide and seek in their house
Trying not to get caught
Climbing the big apple tree in the
Back yard.

Dad marriage
New wife
No fear of losing him
HAPPINESS

Birth of first son
Premonition: must call
Date: October 14ᵗʰ, Thanksgiving
What's his name?
TURKEY

Reading book in bedroom
DODDLE! DODDLE! DODDLE!
Open door, look down
Big smiling face
Peering up at me

Birth of second child
Daughter
Old nanny asks:
What's her name
GILLIAN

Hard time for father
Second wife has a brain aneurism
Eventually dies
Father never lets on
We know that inside he is
Suffering

Years pass
Father sees someone at a big event
They start dating
We meet her on a Christmas skiing trip
In Jasper

Nice woman
Someone to fill the void
In dad's life
Private Marriage
Happiness again

Summer trip to Central America
Glamorous and exciting
Five day tour into the jungle
Scuba diving in Honduras

TRAGEDY

Desperate need of family support
Mother
Dedicated and supportive
Could not have asked for more
Becomes: The Mother

Mother sometimes comes with brother
Adds humour to the situation
Half sister also brings humour
Moms' friend comes with horns on birthday
Pompoms for every occasion

Father reliable and dependable
Even though lives on the other side of the country
Comes to visit
OFTEN

In turn
All family members
Came to visit me in the
HOSPITAL

Michael, Jody, Daniel, and Gillian

Jody's Dad, his wife Maureen, Daniel, and Gillian

Grandma Ann & Grandpa Al

Jody and Sheva

My Brother

I don't remember his ever not being there
He is 18 months younger than I, so I was too young to remember
But my mom shared stories about me in my "terrible two's"
I was old enough to walk, and my brother was in a baby carriage
I seemed to know that my mom wasn't able to move around quickly

I was in my 'running-around-naked' stage, and I thought it was hilarious
I knew it bugged my mom, and this made it even funnier
So I would sneak out of the house completely naked
And call my mom on the way out the door
My mom would take my brother in his baby carriage

And come running after me down the street
We were at the top of a hill, which gave my mom the perfect view
of my little bum running down the street
turning around ever so often to laugh at her
And I would hear wailing screams coming from the baby carriage

From a young age I had a passion for riding horses.
When he was just crawling I thought my brother looked like a horse
I continued riding him until he grew stronger, and bucked me off!
Now he is 6'4" and the thought of my being bigger is funny!

When we were little we both had vivid imaginations
so we played imaginary games together with stuffed animals
We were good about giving each other private playing time
I can still hear the explosion sounds coming from my brother's room
as he played. I was a definite girl, and played barbies without my brother

We went through my parents divorce together, which was especially hard for my mom
We were too young to completely understand, but we always had each other
All of my experiences were with him, and they were quite diverse
From experiences with my parents together and when
they were separated – such as traveling on exciting trips,
to time spent with my grandparents, to our love for our dog,
to our different nannies

Our family life changed dramatically!
My dad remarried, and had 2 more *kids*!
They were a welcome addition and we both love them.
I love kids, so I got to play big older sister!

Unlike most brothers and sisters we always got along
During my difficult teenage years, he was present but silent

during University, I was away in BC and he went to University of Toronto
We did not really talk, but it was comforting to know he was there

After my last year of University I was in a near fatal accident
My mom said that his words were the most comforting. He said,
"If she dies we'll bury Sheava's (my dog for 16 years) ashes with her.
He did not do well when I was in my coma, and failed 3 courses.

I was always the brave one who told stories of my adventures
I had worked hard setting my career goal
And had already started finding work in my area

I knew what I wanted my future to hold BUT
my brother never talked about his future goals
After graduation he was having a hard time deciding what he wanted to do
FINALLY after three years of constantly switching jobs, he found a career path
I was working on finishing my degree at U of T, and every time I went to the library

my brother would be there searching for graduate programs he found interesting
He finally found a combined Law and Forensic Psychology PHD
Now he finally showed how smart he was
Everyone was so proud of him and he was excited

For the first time, I was jealous.
Everyone told me how smart my brother must be.
He reacted with typical modesty
He acted like going to that program was NO BIG DEAL

He always reminds me that he is excelling scholastically, but I am living
Despite what everyone said, "I BEAT THE ODDS!"
Although far away, we chat on MSN regularly
the fact that I have trouble talking doesn't hinder our relationship

I am one lucky girl to have such a special brother in my life
We have been through everything together
I'm happy to say that I now consider him one of my
BEST FRIENDS
I love you Brother 1!

While living in Toronto, I really missed the life I lived in Edmonton where I went to a Hebrew School, and was very proud of my religion. When I moved to Toronto, I lived in a very Jewish area, but I disliked what the people stood for, and I became ashamed. My life revolved around my horse and riding. I became depressed and anorexic. I traveled to France for a summer and decided I loved being away from home. I switched schools to a more structured environment and I loved it. I became obsessed with my grades. My teacher always told me how smart I was and instead of taking it as a compliment, I felt like I had to prove myself. In high school I went to school in Cambridge England for a semester. I came back because although

I wouldn't admit it, I was lonely. When I worked as a riding instructor for a summer and started building up my confidence.

While I was writing my book I received an email from a childhood friend who had been my best friend in Edmonton since grade 1. In my office I have a picture of the two of us taken in my grandparents' backyard in Camrose. We took a bus to their house alone and were very proud of our accomplishment.

Jody & Nadina

I remembered a project about the kibbutz movement in Israel that we wrote together. I did all the research and my friend wrote the notes and illustrated the project. I kept it all this time in my filing cabinet.

The picture and the project triggered many memories and emotions. Memories triggered other memories and I became inspired to write a poem about my childhood and adolescence. As I remembered, I moved forward and backward in time, going off on tangents and coming back again. This movement is reflected in the writing.

Childhood Memories

I am fortunate my best friend from grade 1 remains my best friend
We never fought
Even when it wasn't "cool" to be crazy and care free
She was, and she made me laugh

When we were little each recess
We played on the jungle gym with pretend "animals".
I had a fuzzy girl bunny rabbit named "Fluffy"
Nadina had a skunk named "Flower"
We were not normal children!

Whenever she came over we played "Barbie"
I would make elaborate houses filled with furry furniture
She would make simple houses with minimal furniture
I would then ask her to trade, because I liked hers better

I was an insecure child, and never felt good enough
My greatest fear was to be "alone" and friendless
I never felt this way with her

I knew Nadina from Jewish day school.
From early childhood, religion was always an important part of my life
My grandparents emphasized the importance of my Jewish identity
In Edmonton I felt different and proud of it!
In grade 4 in Toronto

my math teacher told me I would never get into university
Another teacher saw me crying, sent me to talk to the principal
Who heard my story, shook his head
The next day the math teacher apologized
And began to treat me like a princess

I was tested and found to have a spatial learning disability,
Knowing this only gave me more determination
I only wish that I could work as hard now as I did then
Somehow my marks became the most important thing in my life
Report Cards came to measure me as a person

All my classmates wanted to work with me

I did all the research and my classmates made the projects "pretty"
It became important to achieve perfection in everything
Athletics, piano playing, horse-riding
I had no self-esteem!

In grade 6 I became jealous of a girl because she was so skinny
She seemed to be the "apple" of everyone's eye.
In Junior High, I felt very alone.
My fellow students were concerned with looks and clothes
Making sure they were in the "in" group
I was too shy to even talk to the "in" group.
I was considered elitist and self pre-occupied
And felt very alone, like a "loser"

At lunch, I used to sit alone and write Nadina letters.
My care-free childhood buddy helped me to forget all of my worries
This has continued into adulthood.

Blessed Friendship

Newly arrived from Edmonton. Want to pursue your dream of riding!
Started riding in Edmonton in group lessons two a year before.
Joanne had been riding at her cottage every day all summer.
Instant friends with a common new love
New love envelopes entire life

Not alone in new quest
Soon entire life becomes about horses
Manage to be silly and have fun with Joanne
Many funny stories while growing up
COMPLETE GOOFBALLS!

BOUGHT NEW HORSE from her family friend
DEEPLY interconnected!
Go to church with her more than synagogue
she is older, so she DRIVES to barn
take bus to her house after school for drive to barn

Joanne = hard worker
I wanted to escape life in Toronto
Joanne = safe route = University of Toronto vs.
Jody = Needed to escape = UBC
Began to love life = UBC = FREEDOM

Stay good friends while at UBC
Vacation = Toronto = visit = have fun
Joanne = Graduation
Education degree = Hong Kong teach
Adventurous like Jody

Sister of Joanne visits Jody while at UBC
Karen = 5 years older than Jody
Past = too much older
Now = good times
Decision = trip to Central America

Trip = fun, exciting
Scuba diving, trek through jungle
Luxury = Costa Rica
California - tragedy strikes
Driving from Palm Springs to Las Vegas = wind storm
Picks up SUV and flips it 4 times front over back down the highway

Unfortunately Karen hits her head and dies from head trauma immediately after
Jody = coma for 6 months waking up from Post Traumatic Amnesia
Wakes up in Erie, Pennsylvania.
Joanne visits with Fiancé.
Lives in Australia with two sons and husband
Life goes on normally for her
Beautiful life in Australia = mother, teacher
Developed beautiful life of my own = very different

Delayed relationship with Joanne
Now on same page
Understand each other = now same goals as before
Developing relationship over again
Blessed FRIENDSHIP!

Jody with Lena & Joanne with Threat

HIGH SCHOOL

In high school I was very shy and insecure
I had severe problems with accepting myself
I had my first serious boyfriend in grade 10
He was very accepting of me and made me feel like a princess
But that wasn't good enough for me

I became obsessed with popularity, broke up with my boyfriend and became depressed
I got involved with drugs and the "right" crowd
I thought I was cool because my best friend was this "cool" guy
I worried about preserving my image rather than what was good for me
I suddenly realized that I wasn't happy being the me I created

I became obsessed with my weight
I blamed everything wrong in my life on my weight
Soon I became bulimic
My boyfriend was very overweight and to me that was the worst possible thing
I disliked myself so much I decided to commit suicide

I wrote a suicide letter and my mom found it
She was crying when she picked me up from my boyfriend
It seems silly to me now that when you are young your life depends only on the moment
Now I realize that although life can be full of disappointments, life goes on
Especially now I realize that you make your life what you want it to be

*(The realization came to me after my accident when I realized that if I became
depressed about issues I had to deal with, life would not be worth living)*

My mom decided that I needed a new school
I started going to a private school in December of grade 12
I don't know whether she told the principal about my situation
But I did feel cared about and wanted to prove I could do well

At this new school I became obsessed with doing well
Our marks were pasted on the wall for the whole school to see
I especially feel pressured to do well
When everyone knows about how I am doing

I always had trouble when I was stressed
I skipped classes to prepare for upcoming assignments
Because I had to do well, I would spend hours working on assignments
I went to the library every day after school for hours to finish my work
The problem was nothing was good enough

Jody & Vanessa

I graduated from high school and for my undergraduate studies I went to UBC. There I felt as though I had become a new person. I was no longer shy. In my first year I worked out and was on the rowing team. I started liking myself more and entered a relationship with a young man who took care of me, drove me to rowing team practices at 6:00 AM, and was my best friend. I became very involved in Hillel, the Jewish Student Organization at the University, and felt very proud of being Jewish again. I worked in Jasper for the first summer and became more self-confident. Although I did not enjoy my job as a chambermaid, I was well-liked by staff and guests.

The next summer I went on a trip for university students entitled "Anguish to Hope." We visited the concentration camps in Poland and then traveled to Israel. There, my friend and I lived on a kibbutz. One day, I looked out, and saw horses on the kibbutz, and from then onward everyday after I finished my kitchen duty, I went riding. There were a few little girls who came riding with us. Coincidentally, one of the horses was named "Ayelet" which is my Hebrew name. Ayelet means "baby deer." When I returned to Toronto, I was on a talk show speaking about the trip.

The following year I decided I definitely wanted to be a teacher, a dream I nurtured from the time I was a young child. But this was not to be. In one brief moment, my life was altered completely and my plans were put on hold.

Jody & Vanessa in Israel, 1993

CHAPTER 5:

THE ACCIDENT

It is hard to believe that my life was not always like it is today. It all began after a beautiful trip in Central America. It makes me feel better that I can say that without hesitation. Unfortunately, I was not alone on my trip. The friend who was traveling with me died in the roll-over. I was left with a brain injury. In hindsight, our trip was perfect. If there were a suitable time to go, in my books, it would be after a perfect vacation that we shared. I wrote this poem describing our trip. The poem has a fictional ending.

Longed for ending

What didn't happen
Where to start?
Standing by the baggage passing time
wild, crazy adventures of Central America
beyond my imagination
would anyone else believe?

Arrived in Costa Rica
Crisp blue water crashing onto the beach in ferocious waves
Anticipation of adventure

Guides jovial, excitable and full of life
Greeted us with a smile
Made us feel comfortable

Hands flew in every direction
Plans for our time in Costa Rica consumed our guides
Luck on our side
Reserved a luxurious villa near the capital

Zoomed off in a red sports car
Not a moment of silence
Heard plans and suggestions
Excitement filled my body

Was this real or fantasy?
Looked at the side view from the car to learn the truth

Reality of poverty HARSH!
Outside window scrawny children ran barefoot on stony village fields
Guides seemed oblivious to poverty outside window
Ask "why?"… Reply, "Everyone has their own challenges in life."
Strange concept: live life without pity

First adventure: drove through town
Visible how locals struggle for survival
Tourist traps planted in the midst of scenery on a beautiful coast
Could ignore the poverty

Waves huge, people sleeping in hammocks while taking surfing break
Beautiful bronzed muscular bodies of men left me wanting to see more
Guide suggested why not stay?
Laughed at her sudden want
Had to stick to plan, space reserved for us
Had to head on to the "hard life" of a beautiful resort town
Felt guilty about living in such luxury

Luxury became even more apparent as entered the town
Each resort seeming like its own town, beautiful white stucco buildings
Boutiques on the side of road filled with touristy garb
Turned and drove down long driveway to villa
Breathtaking view from cliffs leading down to the ocean below

Walking down stairs from the top entranceway to the pool
Looked cool and fresh, inviting us to dive in
Or sit at the bar at the side of the pool with bar stools in the water
Had to remind myself not wearing a bathing suit
Walked to a small villa of our own to the side of the pool
Shook head in disbelief at the beauty of the green vegetation

The building was a white glowing shrine
Raced to get ready,
could already feel the cool water lapping up against my body
spent all day at the pool soaking up the sun
enjoying feeling spoiled
spent whole excursion in bliss

four days passed, drove back to capital city ready to start new adventure

four days out of three-month trip
thought of explaining three-month trip too tiring
would take a couple of weeks to tell
questions could be answered just by looking at our tans, bags filled
with souvenirs from the markets, scuba diving certificate

Tell guide we had a great time.

Unfortunately, this is not what happened. And when the accident happened, I was not alone. My friend who was with me was killed instantly.

When I woke up from my coma, I did not remember anything. My mom had the unfortunate job of explaining everything to me. She explained well, except originally she did not mention one very crucial fact. For a long time I blamed myself for the accident. It was only years later that I found out that I had a major court case against the car company. Apparently they knew the car I was driving was dangerous, but decided not to take it off the road. Most people die in car roll-overs and car companies are not held responsible. I was fortunate to have excellent lawyers. Also, despite their having to re-live her loss, my friend's family supported me in my fight

After my accident, I was airlifted by helicopter to a hospital in San Bernadino, California where I spent a month in intensive care. I was given one day to live. When my friends talked about flying down at the end of the week to see me, my mom told them they should come as soon as possible because I may not live that long. My boyfriend drove down that day too. He said he held my hand and talked to me hoping to break through.

I think a lot of that time was spent supporting my mother too. Although I was in life threatening circumstances, I was unaware. It was my mother who needed the support. I am and was very close to my mother and would want her to have as much support as possible. Her two sisters and two best friends flew out. My father also came with his wife, even though they live across the country. My mother said he even cried, perhaps because his second wife died of a brain aneurysm, and it was just too much for him to handle.

I wrote this poem when I pieced together my mom's description of how she received news of my accident and came to be with me.

My mom

A bomb hit with one phone call
Your daughter has been in a serious car roll over
Her friend died
We still have to call her friend's parents
We think your daughter is still alive fighting for her life

We think she is your daughter because she is 5'9" and
According to her passport, your daughter is 5'10' and her friends is 5' 3"
We need to know how to get in touch with her father
Is he with you?

He lives in Edmonton. I will call him.
We suggest you come immediately
because we don't know how long she will live.

My mom told my dad to go immediately to San Bernadino
She told the nurses in the hospital to rub my back,
Then she booked her ticket
My dad told my half brother I was fighting for my life
"Kill the person," he told my dad,
not knowing that I was in a single car roll over
My mom and dad arrived on the same day
My mom told me that when my dad saw me in a coma, he cried

Two of my mom's friends and her sisters flew in
My mom called my friends and told them what happened
They wanted to come in a week
My mom told them I might not be alive in a week
They came.

Friends called other friends
My friend who was filling in for me as an autistic therapist
Went around to all my clients, taped them talking, and sent me the tape
Telling me about their progress

Against all odds, I made it, but at that point my mom was told I would never wake up. I was in a coma for the trip back home. We flew in a special jet and my mother always tells me how I "missed out on" the gorgeous male crew who flew us.

When we arrived in Toronto, I was immediately transferred to another hospital. This was the first of many transfers for rehabilitation therapy and the beginning of a long, five-year journey until I was finally capable of living on my own in an apartment. First, I was an inpatient at Western Hospital in Toronto. From there I moved as an inpatient to a rehabilitation hospital in Erie, Pennsylvania in the United States for two years. I came back to Toronto, and was an inpatient at what was then RIT for six months. I then moved into a group home apartment and became an outpatient at the Toronto Rehabilitation Centre. Half way through this time, I was dismissed so I could start living my life. My court case finally came through, enabling me to afford more intensive independent therapy. I received treatment at a neurologically based physiotherapy clinic, found a new occupational therapist and speech pathologist.

I do not remember anything until December 1996, six months after my accident. I was in what is called "Post Traumatic Amnesia." All I know about this time, I learned from the "tear-jerker" recovery stories my mom told me. According to her, I started responding after approximately three months. She told me about the time a friend came to visit me from Vancouver. "Look, your friend is here," she said, and apparently, I turned my head to look. She told me how I laughed when my aunt told a joke. During this time, the doctors decided I would never improve, and wanted to send me to a chronic care hospital. I am lucky that I have a mother with more faith in me than that. Apparently, when they told her their plans for me, her response was, "I don't think so."

Off to Erie Pennsylvania I went. I was still in a coma but responding much more. From that time, I learned that doctors, nurses, therapists, friends and family would always be surprised at my capabilities. I am now accustomed to people doubting everything I decide to tackle. Even back then, my determination came from a state of mind, not something I thought about consciously. I was determined to do well. Unfortunately, at that point, doing well had its limitations. I had to accomplish all I was never supposed to, to gain their belief in me. Some of the staff drove me crazy. For example, I just underwent an operation to lengthen my heel-cords so my feet would not point down like a ballerina. The nurse's aide was giving me a shower, and she made the water so hot that it burnt me. She could not understand my speech. I did not have a talking computer as yet, and she thought I was just whining. I took the nozzle and sprayed her until she was soaking wet. I wonder how I would react now. At the time, my reaction was blamed on my injury. I write about my frustration with communication in this poem.

Communication

Suddenly
A world without communication
Thinking, but being unable to have a conversation
Living without a mode of expressing myself
Frustration

Going from a world full of talking and laughing
To a silent world
ALONE
Knowing why this has happened to me

Understanding how to enter the world I miss
Knowing this is not the battle
It's educating others about this new world I live in

Making others understand
That I am not stupid
After all, in time I will be fluent in two languages
Leaving them in the dust

Starting to learn a new language from scratch
It will be difficult to make signing my primary language

Perhaps even impossible
Considering very few people know it

It will be the only way to make myself equal
To be able to function on the same level as everyone
To know that I fit in

I also had good times at Erie. I made friends with a quadriplegic girl. I remember being jealous that she could talk but decided later that it was better to be like me, and still have the possibility of improvement. I was taken to a concert with her, which was a special treat and great fun. My mother traveled up to a nearby bed-and-breakfast every weekend to prevent me from becoming lonely. A faithful volunteer spent Friday's with me, and for a while, a girl came during the week. I was lucky in that my therapists were all very caring people. I became very close with some and remain in contact with them even now. I was close with my speech pathologist. Speech was the hardest disability to deal with. Therapists were afraid of thinking I could improve and did not want to give false hope. They even stopped therapy, believing improvement was not possible. Like my heel cord operation during my physiotherapy, it took intervention, a change in outlook, for my speech to improve.

The time came when I was ready to leave Erie and return to Toronto to continue therapy. At that point, my speech had not improved sufficiently to be comprehensible. I desperately needed a speech computer. My neuro-psychologist suggested I write a letter to Chedoke in Hamilton requesting permission to return to a rehabilitation hospital in Toronto.

When I first returned to Toronto, the focus in speech therapy was mostly on how to use my light-writer more effectively. My speech disability always bothered me greatly, especially when I wanted to use the telephone, an instrument people use every day to reach others. I express this difficulty and frustration in the poem entitled, "Telephone."

Telephone

Verbal communication: Essential for humanity
"normal" communication impossible for me
Speech difficulty: aphasia, dysarthria, apraxia, deafness
The telephone = an ideal instrument?
Only if barrier free
Tools: light-writer, computer, sign language
It's not easy, but it must be done

Circumstances determine the method used

When I returned to Toronto, I was ready to leave Erie, but I was not ready to be dependent on my mother again. In Erie, I was dependent on her to buy my daily supplies, but I only saw her on weekends. Even at that point, I was making my own lunch once a week. It is funny how proud you become of doing the daily activities that become something you would rather not do when you do not have an injury. Making a meal was a luxury, and I wanted to do my laundry and dishes. In Erie, I remember feeling so proud when they let me do my laundry and took me grocery shopping for the ingredients to make one meal a week. I took that as a sign of recovery.

In my first group apartment, once a week each of us had a turn to prepare a meal for everyone. I had a boyfriend who helped me come to grips with my injury. Towards the end of my stay, I became frustrated, realized I was having trouble concentrating, and broke up with my boyfriend. We remained good friends.

SAVIOUR

It feels strange to call him my saviour, but that's what he was.
He saved my self-esteem. University = very popular with men
Remember going to a movie with my mom while in hospital in Erie, Pennsylvania
Crying: No one could ever like me like this
Would have to be crazy!
Response: You will meet a nice boy who loves your humour and warmth
Whatever!

Get rolled in new apartment, excitement after living in a hospital
Meet everyone. Excited have Kitchen, and a living room with couch and a TV
Even though never watch TV, excited by normalcy
Dinner, everyone new. Gather around the table
One very cute man - David
Haven't met anyone "cute" since accident

Wheeltrans to music group - fun!
Thought: he could never like me! Easy to talk to!
Problem: Does NOT remember.
Remembers the important things = me
Treats me like a queen!

One night at residence, he walks me to my room KISS
He walks, so pushes me everywhere - NOT trapped! Pushes me to a coffee restaurant
"Will you be my girlfriend?" Blushing
YES

Has apartment he shares with other resident
LOTS of quality time. Makes me feel so SMART!!
LIKE he doesn't notice JODY = very DISABLED!!
Fun to be with! Laugh a lot!!
Many of the same interests!! Loves travel and exploring
Everything too good to be TRUE!!

Settlement: move into my own apartment
David comes by bus to visit many times
TRAGEDY- David falls out of bus when driver doesn't stop
Can't visit independently. He now has trouble physically too.
Trouble with balance. Still very caring!

Difficult when I cannot see him alone.
Only visiting group apartment
Or when we go to Swiss Chalet near his apartment!

8 years together. Still care about him!
We break up, but he knows that I will always be grateful for making me feel so special.
Stopping DEPRESSION!!
Always be an IMPORTANT part of my life!

SAVIOUR!!

Jody & David

Everyone decided it was time for me to move out on my own. The settlement of my case against the car company finally came through. In my first meeting with the lawyers for the company, they looked right at me and said it was my fault. Once we reached an agreement, a condition of my settlement with them was that the head lawyer would write me a letter of apology. He wrote me a letter of apology saying that he was sorry if his comments hurt me, but he needed to make them for the sake of the case. I wrote an imaginary response to Fat Mike in the form of a poem.

Fat Mike

I understand your reasoning
Thank you for apologizing
Even though it is not possible to forgive you,
My life is not as horrible as you make out

I lost a great deal
However, I gained a new beginning
Before my accident, my life was planned
With hard work I created a new life

It took determination and perseverance
I must be self advocating
To achieve what I want
People are not pessimists

I realize

Acquiring acceptance is attainable
I no longer have to battle to be believed
I can say "so-long" to the sob story
It's still a sad story, the product of paradox positive

Changes and challenges, my story surrounding solitary strategy
Make the most of every moment
Dilemmas are difficult, but not like a destructive disease
Exploring the environment ends in excitement

Additional adventures arise
Being disabled
becomes distinguishable from being dead
I now am able to live life leisurely

What makes your existence so wonderful?

My mother was "Miss Picky," and it took a while until she finally decided on a suitable apartment. In 2004, I moved out of a 24-hour supervised living apartment for the head injured into my own apartment. It is a huge, beautifully decorated, in a perfect location with incredible facilities. My friend from grade one knows about my passion for pets. So, for my thirty-first birthday she brought me my cat Yo-Yo from the Humane Society. At the moment, I have daily staff to drive me to my activities, clean my apartment, and help me with meal preparation. I have a mouth-piece that helps me talk, and also use a talking computer to make my speech clear.

Jody & Yoyo

Originally my friend's death sapped my energy. Until today, the anniversary of my car roll-over is painful and difficult. On each anniversary I go down to the water of Lake Ontario. I light a candle and put it in the water to float, and say a prayer for my friend. Originally I used to go to church because her mom is a devout Catholic, but I realized that my friend was not and she loved the water. In fact, at her cottage in Muskoka, she would swim in the lake, jump out, wrap herself in a towel and go into the church still dripping wet.

As time passed, because I was living daily with the results, the accident became more about me than her. This may sound selfish, but I wish my friend had lived so I could share my experiences with her. The problem with brain injury is the brain has many diverse functions, so it is impossible to meet someone with the same injury. It is hard to find someone who shares my experiences and struggles. I deal with most of my frustrating situations alone.

My roll-over caused me to change my career plans. During my recovery, I realized that because of my speech problem, hearing kids would not understand me. I decided I needed to learn sign language, because the only kids I could teach successfully were the hearing impaired. I audited my first course with my mother. At that point, I could not see the writing on the board, so my mother had to read it to me. However, in sign language classes, the teachers do not speak. I do not know what I was thinking. If I could not see the board, exactly how was a going to see the students' sign? But I was determined. I finished that class, and decided to go to the Bob Rumball Centre for the deaf for further training. I still had to finish my degree from the University of British Columbia, and my prerequisites for Deaf Education. I figured I would become a teacher when I was ninety!

My journey has been and still is long, lonely and hard. Unfortunately, since my injury, obstacles prevent me from completing my dreams and plans. One of the obstacles I face is trying to become a teacher of children with special needs. For this type of work, I need accurate speech and mobility. I no longer have either of these essential abilities. At times, I feel depressed and despondent. I express these feeling in the following poems:

Life

How do I like myself
Given all my new barriers?
It's difficult
Most of the time I want to CRY

People comment on how great my family
Is for supporting me
I agree. They are great
But no one every considers how it feels to me ME

I guess begging for attention
Is far from admirable
I just want to be treated like the same person

Externally I am different but inside I'm not
Learning about the life of those
Less fortunate than I
Makes me realize how lucky I am

Thinking of the horrible stories
In my Holocaust class
Makes me feel selfish
For not enjoying every moment of the life I have

Does this sound like a sob story?
It's easy to get wrapped up in your own MISERY
And miss the fact that in essence
I have an incredible life

Time

Time has passed
life is not what I had expected
Is the difference so horrible?
I must let go of old self expectations.
it's still possible to like myself even though old goals are no longer realistic

I've built a new life
very different to the old one
I've made new goals
I strive to conquer
what others say is impossible

eleven years after the accident
life has drastically changed
I've picked up old pieces,
tried to rebuild my life
I have a successful solution so far

In class not even thinking, I write down a date
I look down, surprise:
to my astonishment according to the paper it is 1996
For the past eleven years that year
has represented the grand finale

Time to rethink!
Maybe it was a grand finale to one life
and the beginning of another
I have to decide what is attainable
I must STRIVE TO ACHIEVE

Down in the Dumps

Down in the Dumps

Is this a normal reaction?
To what?
That's the question

Having a difficult day
Everything in my life feels wrong
It hurts to walk
Told to ask my therapists for advice

I know the answer
No No No
Everything you enjoy
Is bad for you in some way

Which leads to the next question:
What do you enjoy that
Can be good for you?
Is what you're *feeling* the real problem

Or does the real problem have a longstanding history?
Is the issue stress, or is everything piling up?
The real problem is loss of control!
It's UNMANAGEABLE

The key to success is
One step at a time
Tomorrow during the day
I will try to deal with school

Try to separate my personal life
As much as possible
It's not going to define who I am
As a person

If anything I will become
Stronger for dealing with my reality
So focus on making myself
A unique individual I can be proud of

They say I'm an inspiration
So start acting like one
If they're going to make statements about me,
Then I have to prove they're right

CHAPTER 6:

GIVING BACK

Since my accident, I decided I was not happy always taking and never giving, so I started my volunteer work with kids with special needs and those who are not cognitively sound.

I decided to learn sign language and teach the hearing impaired. I audited my first course with my mother, and then went to the Bob Rumball Centre for the deaf for further training. As my sign language improved, I chose to volunteer at a local children's hospital with a deaf girl who has cerebral palsy. She has problems with communication, does not have fine motor skills, and uses her head to communicate. She has trouble keeping her weight down, so I encouraged her to exercise at the gym. We continue to do many activities together. I also began working with an autistic girl teaching her sign language, but I found this very hard without the use of speech. Like me, she is also in a wheelchair because she has mild CP. When I volunteer with her, it is like she is my teacher, not that I am hers.

After I completed Sign Language Level III, I decided to volunteer at the deaf daycare. Initially I was turned down. The interviewers claimed that because I was disabled, I would be unable to work with kids. My disability was especially problematic in the deaf world where the kids do not have speech. They believed the kids needed someone without a physical disability. Much to my surprise, and after much persuasion, I was eventually accepted. Some of the kids are deaf, but in many ways, those that are deaf are ahead of those who are not. One girl in particular is ahead and smarter than most of the hearing kids. I cannot tell that she is deaf. She picks up on what the other kids are doing and follows right along. The other kids do not treat her as though she is different. The teacher was surprised that on my first day the children all wanted to walk with me and hold my hand. They did not realize that I cannot walk. Sometimes I "read" picture books to them. I take the books home to practice reading them in sign language in which I have become quite proficient. I sometimes choose books for them from the library.

The truth is, some days, I have what I call "feeling sorry for myself days." I allow myself one every month. One day, at the daycare centre I felt very discouraged. Life seemed unfair. Mostly, I am still a little kid at heart. I love to climb on the play set or slide down the slide with the children. And there was this tooth brushing activity. The kids had to scrub hard boiled eggs that had spent the night in Pepsi Cola with toothbrushes and toothpaste, when I tried getting down on the floor with them, I slipped. Not a big deal, but I felt embarrassed.

I seem to always work with the kids that are behind the others in terms of development. There is one girl who is physically and cognitively delayed, as well as deaf. I loved working with her, seeing her face light up when I took her for a ride in my chair. She particularly liked it when I stopped in front of a ball and we kicked it together.

Since my injury, working with the disabled or less fortunate helps me realize how lucky I am. I write about my experiences with children in the following poems:

Childhood love

I tell my mom it's not a job
I get to play
She tells me it may be play to me
To others it's work
I have never considered
Playing with kids work

What I find difficult
Are my shortcomings
In this line of work

It is embarrassing when three-year-olds
Know the language better than I

That is what learning is all about
It is important not to forget
That children acquire new languages
More easily than adults

I also find my disability frustrating
I cannot chase after them in the sandbox
All the things I remember enjoying as a child
Seem very difficult for me

Children that age also have a short attention span
This is difficult for me
Because I move slowly

Given all my complaints
What is comes down to
Is my love of children

Seeing their faces light up
When doing something fun or exciting
For me, makes it all worthwhile

Simplicity of childhood

Screaming, laughing, blocks falling from the fort the children built
Bikes zooming by from a bike race in the gym
The noises of childhood excitement

Entering the gym, seeing the children come running
Big smiles on their faces, full of laughter
Inner pleasure, such small events can provide so much happiness

Children offer so many ACCEPTANCES
Knowledge that many of them cannot hear
The noises so familiar, children playing, childhood excitement

Momentary sadness followed by shame
Open your eyes - These children do not know they are different
The hearing kids have adapted and are trying to accommodate any way possible

Instantaneous misunderstanding about how to behave is over
Enough serious stuff, time to play again
From a child's perspective, grown ups are so silly

Why waste playtime worrying about how to behave
Treating everyone as an equal makes much more sense
That way no one feels bad

I wrote the poem below after a university poetry class discussion of Keats's poem entitled "Autumn." Keats describes the beauty of the season of autumn. He died of tuberculosis at a very young age, and "Autumn" is said to be an elegy to himself. Watching children play in the autumn leaves reminded me of Keats's poem, and I wrote the following:

AUTUMN

Bright, fresh, colourful smell of nature
the feeling of freedom comes with fall
long to jump into the pile of freshly raked leaves
in the yard

see children playing
hide and seek in the leaves
the child thinks he is so well hidden
forgets about the BIG
bulge his presence makes in the pile of leaves

his pals prancing by the pile prepared to pounce
sounds of screams and shrieks
as the friendly souls slide into the solitary figure
supposedly sneakily hidden

Fancy, fun interpretation of fall forgets that in fact
it is a FINALE
hot heat ends in heartfelt beauty
Is this an elegy
to a terrific life?

Death is disturbing, writing your own elegy is difficult
Keats managed to maneuver this masterpiece magnificently
by surreally sketching the season Autumn as self
a bright, beautiful depiction of his life

TERMINATING

Paulina

Entire life about making a difference in children's life
Worked in many elementary schools
Couldn't find my niche
Loved working with children, wanted to be of help
Saw advertisement in Psychology department

Working with Autistic children helping with communication
Completely unexplored territory for me
Took job helping child with everything
Expressive, Receptive language, toileting etc.
Pre-school, skating, swimming, playgrounds
Horseback riding, bowling

Close with family
When went on vacation - friend took over
Tragedy - in hospital in coma
Finally - trip to Vancouver
Family treats me like long lost treasure

Still close with family and Paulina many years later

A visit with Paulina in Vancouver, BC

Most recently, in order to get into a teaching program, I volunteered at two schools, McKee and Sunny View Public Schools. McKee is a regular school whereas Sunny View is a school for disabled children. I have learned and grown from these experiences. At McKee, I volunteered in a grade1/2 classroom. I loved it. I found the experience more educational for me as the setting was more academic. I was able to help the children in academic areas such as reading, math, grammar, punctuation, and even in religion. I gave the children spelling tests with my light-writer while covering up the front. I taught them not to be ignorant of people with disabilities. The teacher taught the lesson at the front of the classroom and then chose those who have trouble with the work to come to me at the table at the back of the classroom for extra help. They all wanted to work with me if they could. An example was a grade one girl who was moved to my classroom because of a "behaviour" problem. She had great difficulty grasping concepts and I worked with her for a long time. I loved it. She was very attention seeking, but once I got her to understand, she was very excited about learning. She understood why 7 + 3 = 10, but she could not understand why 70 + 30 = 100. When I helped her to understand the concept, she became very excited. Academically, that was the most exciting moment of the week. But what thrilled me the most were the letters the children wrote to me at the end of the week. There was one letter in particular that was so special. One child wrote, "Dear Jody, We're going to miss you. I know you'll be a good teacher. Even though you're in a wheelchair. I love you. I know you're a good person." This letter made me realize that I am teaching something by being who I am.

For my Educational Assistant Course I had a placement in a Catholic public school where I worked two days a week. I worked in small groups with children with behaviour problems, children who were disruptive to the rest of the class. There was one boy in particular who left me struggling, challenged, and doubtful about how to teach. I wrote a poem about him, about how initially he responded to my suggestions, but eventually lost interest. Here is the poem:

Teacher??

Easy to pretend that I don't care, but the fact is I am different
silly to pretend that the children I work with will not notice
Impossible not to notice that I don't walk or talk properly
Changeable? Unfortunately it will always be obvious
Should I give in and change life goal?

Stubborn part of me says NO WAY!!!
realistically, will I ever be truly successful?
It is true that sometimes with kids I just seem to click.
Sometimes kids just seem to know what buttons to push.
How can I get through?

Working at school for my EA placement
different than previous volunteer positions
before teacher always present, so children on best behaviour
trouble-maker behaviour problem of the class always sent to me
reason? I was the only one who could make him work

At first very responsive to my positive reinforcement
Figured out my ploy
dare him to do work, say it's very hard
so may not be able to finish
he used to say, "give me 5 minutes"

He would finish and be all proud of himself
Now no longer cares
can't feel good to always be told how bad you are
has to be a way to make him feel "cool" for good behaviour

always says what he knows we want to hear
Today I explained if he could be good for one day
he could participate in everything
could tell from his teacher's reaction that she knew he would say, "yes"
and not comply

Today he made fun of his teacher talking
She took away his recesses, and his gym, and his carnival activities
he has only negative reinforcement
has to be some benefit from positive reinforcement
how can I make him crave positive reinforcement not keep trying for negative

Not a bad kid, actually very intelligent
how can I make him work, and still get the attention he is craving?
Maybe revert it to positive attention

maybe reward with an activity he enjoys
but what about his negative behaviour

maybe ask him how the school could reward him
besides being able to do all the daily activities
maybe he wants to have his class play a weekly game of basketball
The kids would enjoy his reward as much as he.
Let's take it one week at a time, so it's not overwhelming

Make him think he's responsible for giving the class a treat
It may not have to be basketball, but just a weekly play time
That way he would know that the whole class was enjoying his treat
This seems to be the ultimate reinforcement for him.

I would not have spent this much time worrying
if I was not a born
TEACHER

I have included testimonials given to me by the teachers with whom I worked in various settings over the past few years.

June 28, 2006 9:24 PM

Hi Jody, I know I won't see you for a while, as school is almost over and then we have a long summer ahead of us. I just want you to know that we really meant what we said. Please come back to us in September, and we'll do everything in our power to help you find what you want. I know I haven't always been much help - sometimes I feel so helpless because I'm a fairly new teacher and I don't know that much about finding jobs and what not. However, Julio and Claudia (the lady who spoke to you today) are fantastic and very experienced. They will find a way to help you figure out your career path. I know they will. I just hope that I haven't let you down. I know I'm not that helpful, but if I had more power or knowledge, I would help you in a heartbeat! I think you are absolutely incredible, and like I told you today, I am constantly telling people how amazing I think you are. You have more strength in your little finger than most people have in their whole bodies (including me!). Please don't give up, and don't let the world get you down. Be persistent and be pushy, and you will get what you want. I just know it. If there is anything I can do, please let me know. I am here for you and will help you in any way I can. Take care of yourself, and thank you so much for coming into our classroom and brightening our days. The kids adore you, and they just light up when they see you. You have a true gift, and you need to use that. Take care,Love, Jessica O'Malley

January 16 2008

To Whom it may concern;

I first met Jody Schloss in the fall of 2007 at McKee School. She was interested in finding another volunteer placement for this school year. She began to participate within our Home School Program in the mornings. The students in this group have been identified as exceptional, and are all performing at less than their respective grade levels in most curriculum areas, especially language and math. Our ten children present with a wide variety of learning disabilities and styles.

Jody was enthusiastic about this particular group of students, because she was interested in special Education and Disability Studies. She has responded very positively to any on -the - spot information sessions and follow- up discussions concerning these wonderful children. She is keen to assist them in any endeavor they attempt, always cheerfully and cooperatively, demonstrating intelligence and sensitivity, and a sense of humour (always a plus)!

The students in turn, have responded very warmly to Jody, and her magical keyboard with which she is able to communicate to others. It is especially gratifying to witness both adults and children slow down to the much calmer rate of interaction and real connection that Jody employs. Patience, eye contact, body language, facial expression, and listening skills - as well as reading - are all fundamental to talking with Jody. These are all skills with which the children struggle every day, and Jody invites these young learners to demonstrate their individual abilities and interactive styles in a positive light. This gentle, real, human connection to her as another human being is very important for these students.

For her part, Jody has proven to be game for almost anything going on within our program! She is able to join in with any formal teaching/learning task and assist any student(s) to complete seat work, answer questions, do research, play games, or most importantly, to talk with young people so that they feel important.

Jody is always ready to try new activities, and thoroughly enjoys playing board games as much as helping out with math problems. She has been staying longer in our classroom of late, and has joined the staff for lunch, chatting with other teachers comfortably. She brings a warm and wonderful perspective to our small group, and we have all been enriched by her presence. She is eager to continue her formal education in the area of Disabilities Studies, and we at McKee can attest to her being a most suitable candidate for such a course of action. She would be a strong advocate for special education students, and a wonderful addition to any school, especially one that specializes in the unique characteristics of students with significant difficulties that sometimes impede learning.

We all wish her to best, and certainly want to know what happens next in the life of this wheeling woman warrior!!!

Most sincerely (and with feeling!)

Suzanne McClennan,

CHAPTER 7:

TRAVELS AND HOBBIES

Besides volunteering, I love to travel, and have not allowed my disability to get in the way. I enjoy experiencing other cultures and seeing how people live. Among the places I have visited are Poland, Israel, Central, North and South America, parts of Canada, South Africa and Thailand.

Jody in Thailand, 2004

Jody and her tour guide in Thailand

Jody & Vanessa in Thailand

I went to school in Cambridge, England and Niece, France, and also traveled through Europe and Egypt during my school breaks.

While I was at university, I took a memorable trip through the concentration camps in Poland and then on to Israel. The trip was called "From Anguish to Hope." I wrote two poems my experiences. The first was written while visiting the concentration camps.

Anguish

Not knowing what to expect
Or what my reaction might be
Learning about the atrocities that occurred
Is different than being in the place where they occurred

Seeing for yourself
The sickening conditions under which
People were forced to struggle for survival

The horrible emptiness in the pit of your stomach
Knowing that you are standing
Where
Dreadful nightmares occurred

Being with someone
Who was there
Seeing her stand tall and strong
At a huge pile of human ashes

Knowing that inside she was suffering
Asking her what she was feeling
Hearing the strange response, "At peace."
Staring at her in puzzlement

Why? Finding the answer
In the next sentence

My parents were murdered here
This is their burial site

After spending some time in Israel, I wrote the following poem:

Peace

I do not think that going to the home of my people
Would be hard or leave me with unanswered questions
I had a strong bond with the place and what it represented
It was also a beautiful country with lots to do and see

Upon arrival
A gentle feeling of belonging came over me
People were in a rush to go where they had to go
Yet despite the mad chaos
I felt at peace

I got off the plane, ready for a new adventure
There was a sign with my name in Hebrew lettering on it
I walked slowly towards it
Nervous about what the initial reaction

Of the mother of the children
I would be taking care of for a year
She was gracious and excited as I approached
Encircling me in her arms, and kissing me on the cheek

I walked with her to her car
And was shocked by the depth of affection
I felt for this stranger

In the car she talked about her three children
She bragged and boasted about them
They seemed almost greater than life

When I met them, I knew I had made the right choice to come
Watching them with their mother and father
It was obvious that this was a family
With strong foundations in love

When I asked the mother
Why they would rather give up their precious land
Than have a war
Her answer was plain and straightforward

For peace we would do anything

It's our children who are out there
We will do anything to ensure their survival
They only thing that can guarantee they will be safe is
PEACE

I showed Ariella a video of myself, a teacher, and a fellow student being interviewed on a television talk after our trip. Ariella felt grateful to me for sharing that tape with her, and wrote a journal entry about it, which she gave to me. Let me share it with you.

Anguish to Hope - Jody's trip to Poland and Israel in 1993

It was an experience to see Jody on the screen so beautiful, whole, thick curly brown hair all the way down her back, bright eyes, swinging earrings, beautiful mouth, strong eye-brows, tall, slim, strong looking. Her voice too was strong, tenor, not too high and not too low. She looked poised, confident and graceful between her male fellow traveler and contemporary, the teacher who led the group, and the interviewer, the only female, but fully in control of the situation and uninhibited.

At all times she was so in touch with the moment - with her ideas, with the questions being asked of her, and the experiences themselves. I found her comments profound, wise, articulate, and in terms of her own life in retrospect, so ironic. For example, she spoke of Anna, a holocaust survivor who accompanied the group, as a woman whose strength was immediately recognizable. "With her strength, she could go through anything," Jody said. She commented that Anna told stories so boldly, answered questions without hesitation. I loved Jody's comment on stories. She said that the stories made the experience and the camps believable, the spot where the ashes sat in a container became people, real people who had been through the experience. Jody said what made her terribly sad was that while she, Anna, and the other members of the group were standing in the camps of the Holocaust, remembering and saying that this should never happen again, killing was continuing in Bosnia and other parts of the world. She also commented on seeing Polish school children visiting the camps, riding through them as if they were in a playground. She wondered what their teachers had told them of these camps.

When Jody spoke about Israel it was with depth and understanding of the situation. She spoke about wondering how Israeli's were prepared to give up land, for example Gaza, for the sake of peace. When she stayed on Kibbutz, she discovered the answer. She said, "I understood why they would do anything for peace." She understood that no Israeli wanted to send his/her child, sibling, or parent to fight and possibly get killed.

The ultimate irony for me came when the interviewer asked Jody, "How has this experience changed you?" She answered, "I realized how horrible things can be and how my troubles are so minute by comparison." (Damelin, July 7, 2004)

After my accident, just before Ariella starting working with me, I went on a trip to South Africa. I wrote a poem about the experience.

South Africa

Long time planning expensive adventure
Itinerary for trip jam packed
Traveled with old friend, best friend
Only way to assure mother of my safety

Talked on plane
Realized many things have changed
But friendship has not
Chatted with young boy on the plane
Still had a knack with kids

First: visit to a safari to see wild animals
Three hours from Johannesburg
Drove up: driver got out
People brought out luggage to the tent

End of November, boiling hot
Waited for other group members at pool, swam
Saw water hole in the distance
Two elephants came down to drink
Different world, safari

Traveled by jeep through the game park
Saw lions gnawing on carcass of freshly killed zebra
Tourists jumped out to take pictures
Loud yell came from guide, "No way!"
Drove on and saw other animals
giraffes, buffalo, rhinoceroses, more lions, cougars

Drove back to lion killing, hyenas had taken over
Drove to river opening, saw water shooting up in the air
Discovered large plump shape in the water
Look closer,
Hippopotamus
Unbelievable day, never thought it possible

Kept journal, recorded everything
When having a boring day, could look at it and say, "I have lived!"

Jody & Vanessa in South Africa

I have always loved the water. When my car rolled over, I was on the rowing team at UBC. After my accident, I learned about disabled sailing and heard great things about the disabled sailing club. The thought of being in control of my own boat was exciting! I started sailing when I first moved out of the hospital into the group apartment. To begin, we sailed in a group of about seven sailors. The first time we went out on the water I remember looking around and thinking, this is freedom. I have always been fairly adventurous and love doing exciting things. I thought this was a way in which I could have fun safely despite my disability. I joined the club after my first year. After two years, the instructors decided I was too independent to continue to sail with a group. I am now able to sail with a companion to help out if I get in trouble. Sailing has made me realize that I am still human, and despite my disability, I can still do fun and exciting things. It gives me pleasure and a feeling of independence. Here is an excerpt from the letter I wrote in order to fundraise for our sailing club. It reflects how I feel while I participate in the sport and how important it is for those who are disabled.

Disabled Sailing Association of Ontario
1 Stadium Road
Toronto, Ontario
M5V 3H4

I am writing on behalf of Disabled Sailing Association of Ontario. As many of you may know we have had financial difficulties in the past, but we have managed to get them under control in order for the program to survive. We will be able to make the program survive, however, this year one of our main sponsors has stopped supporting us, due to another program it has decided to participate in. We would not only like to survive, but to prosper and grow while creating new activities for our clients.

For the disabled community, sailing brings a new-found freedom for those who have been restricted mobility-wise for their entire life. It is an exhilarating rush to explore the waters at incredible speeds with the wind gliding through our hair. To those who have spent their lives in a group home, it is a new kind of freedom to suddenly experience something that many able-bodied people long to experience. It is a time when they are not outsiders looking in, but a time that they belong, and can be proud of who they are and their accomplishments.

For those disabled due to an unfortunate accident after birth, such as myself, it brings back the exhilarating rush of an exciting sport we thought we had lost forever. On the water I forget that I am disabled and enjoy the feeling of freedom.

Many pursue the sport competitively. It allows for those who were competitive to maintain their competitive spirit, and for those disabled from birth it encourages competition. (2006)

I also love to ski and go on skiing vacations with my dad who lives in Edmonton, Alberta. We go to Banff or Whistler, and recently, I was in Colorado. Being adventurous is part of me. I never feel afraid when I ski. In fact, the only time I feel scared during a physical activity is when I am walking. At physiotherapy everyone is trying to give me support so they walk with me. I do not have anything to hold on to and feel as though I will fall. Their hands are on my trunk, but for me, this is very scary. When I walk, I see the floor and I feel unsteady. When I ski, I feel empowered, free.

Sit-skiing on Mt. Washington on Vancouver Island

Downhill Temperature

Frozen beauty
Key Word - frozen
Lack of sensation in fingers and toes
All thought focused on coldness

Breathtaking view
White snow flakes covering green trees
The mountain peaks disappearing out of sight
Striking vision

Despite the beauty
All thought focused on the freezing temperature
The white and the distant mountain tops
Racing beside you as you whiz by on your skis

The adrenalin rush from the speed, height, and the beauty
Amongst which you are
Seems to have warmed your chilled body and aching bones
A moment of complete bliss

Winter Wonderland

December 25, 2004
Marmot Basin
Jasper National Park
Alberta, Canada

Winter Wonderland
Unbelievable beauty
Watching the snowflakes
Fall on the people
Screaming, laughing and smiling

Don't forget to open your eyes
To the green of the trees
And witness the beautiful white
flakes on the branches
ready to fall like a soft powder
on the ground
Look at the faces
Of the people skiing down
With big smiles
From an adrenalin rush

SADNESS
Recollection
That once it was you

You are sitting with people
That love you
They want to see you smile
Like you used to do
So naturally

Remember life is what you make it
No one can decide what
You are capable of but you
You time is coming
So HOLD TIGHT

But watching others also reminds me of my disability, of what I was like before my accident, how my friends have moved on, what I have lost. I reflect on this in my poetry.

Old Friendships

Comfort
Celebrating exciting changes
Hearing the gossip
Relaxation

Enjoying their accomplishments

Knowing that you will always be
ACCEPTED
Your accomplishments
No matter how small
Will always be
CELEBRATED
Any excitement you feel with be shared

Much time has passed
Development and changes
Have occurred to
EVERYONE

Don't be selfish
This is about
More than you

Take time to relish and enjoy
The new changes

Sylvia, Vanessa, Jody, Tanya, & Kim

Horseback riding has always been one of my passions. Recently I participated in the Para Olympic Equestrian Championships and won a trophy for the most Sportsmanlike rider.

ONTRA competition in Kitchener, ON

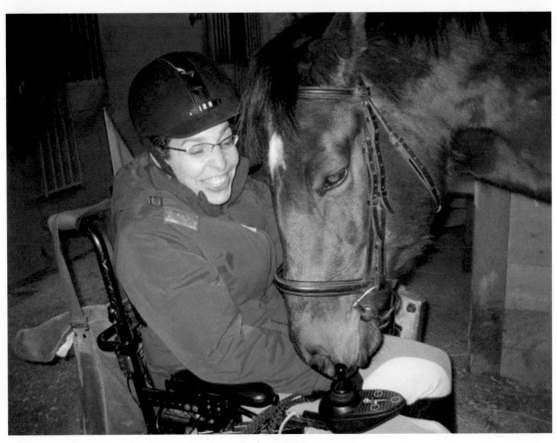

Jody & Dyna

In September of 2006, I traveled extensively and had many adventures. I went sky diving in Vancouver, to a friend's wedding in Muskoka, and to New York City. I describe my experiences in journal entries.

Skydiving: Vancouver, September 12, 2006

I found the experience beautiful and relaxing. I was not afraid at all except for right before I jumped because it looked so high.

I went up in a plane in Pitt Meadows, British Columbia. I was given a jumpsuit and a leather cap. I went tandem with an instructor because I could not land on my own. Before we jumped, in the plane he kept saying things like "breathe deeply" to calm my nerves when I looked down. A cameraman flew with us and came down at the same time. He was so relaxed and made me laugh as we came down by telling jokes. Time went by so slowly. I think we were 1200 feet high. We fell free fall for about 1 minute. It was beautiful. Then the instructor opened the parachute. He kept trying to make me calm by saying things like, "Look at the parachute. Isn't it pretty?" My ears really hurt, so he told me to plug my nose and breathe out. I did this, and my ears popped. I had to do this all the way down. At first, I crossed my arms and held them close to my body. The instructor told me to open them wide and arch my back into a banana shape. It hurt, but I did as he told me.

It was quiet, except for the cameraman who kept talking and joking. The experience felt like it lasted an hour, but it was probably 5 minutes.

While I was in Vancouver, I went back to UBC to visit my old residence. I felt very upset and cried. I also attended a dinner at the Vancouver Yacht Club. The mayor, who is a quadriplegic, was there. I was introduced to him and spent some time talking to him. He tried to give me his attention but was constantly interrupted by people coming up to talk to him. He needed time to understand me or wait for my light-writer, and he did not have that time. People believe that being a quadriplegic is the worst kind of injury. The truth is, the mayor can speak. If you are not heard, you do not have a voice.

My friends' wedding in Muskoka: September 16, 2006

My friend whom I met at UBC, got married on the weekend in Muskoka. She lived in Whistler and for the past four years, I spend time there with her and her husband. She is a physiotherapist and her husband works as a lawyer. My friend and I lived together one summer at UBC, and I saw her regularly. She was my sushi buddy. According to her, I even made my own sushi.

The wedding was in Bracebridge. My friend loves natural beauty and wanted to get married in a scenic setting. She came to the Chuppah on a boat, then walked to the Chuppah where the groom was waiting for her. She told me that she almost fell into the lake while she was stepping out of the boat. The wedding was outside beside the water at a golf club. Her dress was beautiful. I went up on Saturday with another friend who organized everything for me. We met when she was my worker. I came home on my own by bus.

The wedding, though beautiful, was also tinged with sadness. My friend kept telling me about all my men. She joked about the fact that I had too many to know what to do with. Actually, I have no one right now, and that is hard for me. Though everyone was very accepting of me, I felt it was almost in a patronizing way. Perhaps that's just me because as I looked around, I saw how everyone had moved on. I don't feel I have done anything with my life. My friend is marrying, and she has the career she has always wanted. I noticed how different we have become. I am very focused on my goals, but I don't think about my social life in the same way. Before my accident, I would be the one suggesting we go out and she would stay at home to study. Now she has reached her career goal and can go out without worrying. The tables have turned. When she invites me out, I tell her I have to swim and focus on my schoolwork.

New York: September 4, 2006

Amazing!!! When we got to New York it was raining. We stayed at the Roosevelt Hotel where my grandparents courted and saw a jazz singer. It is an old, but renovated hotel. We drove around in a cab. We went for dinner and saw "Sweeney Todd." My relative recommended it. It was good, but I was so tired. New York is beautiful.

My friend works there for the NHL and was our guide. He took us to a Brazil Street Fair on Sunday and we walked around. Then he took us to the Rockefeller Centre which is right opposite the building where he works. We went to the top of the Centre and had a beautiful view of the whole city. Then we saw "Drowsy Chaperone." The show was fantastic. However, the theatre was not accessible. I had to walk up four flights of stairs, and then down again at the end. We had dinner at the Radisson Hotel in Time Square, from where we had a wonderful view of the area. We also took a cab to the Staten Island ferry and climbed on board. I stood on the edge of the ferry and watched. We passed the Statue of Liberty. She is beautiful.

I love New York. The shopping is amazing. We went to the MOMA. We ate Indian food and blintzes at a deli. The portions were huge. Everywhere was accessible, even the taxis. Many of them are tall so my wheelchair fitted in. Also, the taxi drivers are extremely helpful.

Why do I love to travel? Are these travels a search for myself, a search for acceptance? In my poem, I explore that question.

Acceptance

I was born into a prosperous family
I was deeply loved
I never doubted that

I was told that I did not have to prove anything
For some reason I never felt adequate

I always felt I had to show I was worthwhile

I was very shy
I did not feel I was good enough
My life revolved around trying to be accepted

I did not accept myself
I always wanted to be more than I was
I started looking for anything that was stopping me
From being more

I blamed my weight
I soon became obsessed with solving my problem
Soon all my problems could be blamed on my weight

I never realized that
In order to be accepted I had to accept myself first

I went away to university
And found myself in love with my surroundings
It never occurred to me that the reason
Was a change in my attitude not my environment

I remained oblivious to this
Until through no choice of my own
I was forced to move back to where
The difficulties in my life originated

It was here that I discovered that I liked myself
For who I was, not what I was
This was the beginning of my ACCEPTANCE

I continue to travel at any opportunity I am given. Recently I went on a cruise through Central America, and there are other places in the world I have yet to see.

CHAPTER 8:

GRANDPA HYMIE BALTZAN

While writing the story of my life, my beloved grandpa, my mom's father, died on June 2, 2006 at the age of 93. I was the last person to see him alive that Friday night. He passed away at 10:00 PM. I kissed him on the head, something I never did before because he was my grandpa and I thought this was disrespectful.

He spent the last two years of his life at Baycrest where I visited him every week. My grandma Celia, also 93, visited him every day. I am concerned about my grandma. How will she keep herself busy? She and my grandpa were living for each other. She still plays bridge, does needlework and knits despite having trouble with peripheral vision. She has friends in the building in which she has lived since she moved from Edmonton 16 years ago.

Grandma Celia

My grandparents moved to Toronto to be near their children. They had a unique and loving relationship that lastd 67 years. I have written a poem to try to capture my understanding of how they related and felt about each other.

True Love

A 93 year old man says that his marriage has lasted so long because of
LOVE
He says they love each other
Very few people are as lucky as he

Marriages don't last simply because
people don't realize that someone has willingly
devoted his or her entire life to them
they don't realize how important they are to that one other soul

People need to take the time to fall in love
LOVE doesn't mean simply saying, "I love you"
It means
Being prepared to do anything for your "other half"

You have fallen in LOVE
when not being with your love for one day
feels like an eternity
You count the seconds until you can see your love again

They say "your other half" mockingly
but I don't feel complete without her by my side

She makes me feel complete
I only hope that I can make her feel whole too

Getting OLD is the hardest thing I've ever done
My love is my definition of perfect
I never want to be left without my love
and I don't want her to be left without me!

We are the definition of
TRUE LOVE

In one of my courses at university I wrote a paper entitled *The Story of Jacob Baltzan – Pioneer Educator.* In it I tell the life story of my great-grandfather, Jacob Baltzan, a refugee who fled persecution, army service and poverty in Russia to seek a new life in North America. His experience mirrors that of many Jews who were forced to leave their homelands and come as immigrants and pioneers to North and South America at the turn of the twentieth century. Jacob Baltzan got his papers by obtaining a certificate from a doctor saying he was ill and required treatment outside the country.

Towards the end of his life, my grandpa, Hymie Batzan, Jacob's son, fell and broke his hip. He underwent surgery but knew he would never walk again. During my grandpa's last weeks, I wrote a poem which I believe capture him as a person and as a grandfather. My cousin read it out loud on my behalf at his funeral.

Grandpa

When thinking of stories to tell about Grandpa
I always end up laughing or with a big smile
When thinking of stories to tell about him alone,
Somehow Grandma always gets mixed up in the story

I think his worker described him best when he said
SWEET MAN
Very loving, caring
Always made me laugh

Chris told me that when Grandma came to visit
He told Grandpa that his wife was there
And a big smile came over his face
They are my definition of true love.

When my worker asked him:
"What is the secret to a long marriage?
Without even thinking, he said, "love"
Grandma whispered, "It's because I'm the boss."

We thought he was sleeping,
but that created a big smile
He always taught me that with LOVE
you can overcome anything

In my childhood, I spent a lot of time with Grandpa and Grandma
They were my second parents
Grandma was definitely the chef of the household
But whenever I slept over I could count on a good breakfast
made by the chef extraordinaire

I get very stressed about school
being with my grandparents had a magical soothing effect
I sought them out for peace
when on vacation in Palm Springs

At 13 I went to visit them in Arizona
I remember being so proud that I traveled all by myself
Grandpa was always ready for a walk
We explored their area in Scottsdale by foot

My grandparents taught me to be proud of my religion
when I was little on the high holidays
I had the important job of braiding Grandpa's tallit
I don't know if he ever unbraided it or if he just kept a very creative tallit

They made Judaism something more than simply a religion
It came to be associated with family and a warm feeling of belonging
In University I was a very active member of Hillel
I remember thinking, "my grandparents will be so proud."

Since Grandpa has been at Baycrest
I have been visiting him regularly
people say "Isn't that nice of you."
The truth is I did it more for me than for him

Ever since my accident, I have trouble with self worth
Grandpa not only made me feel loved but he remembered my past
An important part of me that I no longer have
And he's always made me feel special for what I have become

He's also very PROUD of my
ACCOMPLISHMENTS that I don't regard as accomplishments
like finally finishing my degree
he bragged to anybody and everybody around

Grandpa loved telling me the story about how when I was little
I used to go to their apartment with a big bag of stuffed animals
I made him tuck in and say good night to each one individually
before I would let him kiss me good night and go to sleep

In the hospital, I brought him two stuffed animals
One with a big smiley face that my friend brought me to cheer me up
The other was a cat
Grandpa told me he loved cats. I wanted to bring Yoyo
but we didn't think the hospital would allow that

The cat was placed in the coffin so that he would not feel alone.

I love you Grandpa
You will always be the best Grandpa that anyone could have

CHAPTER 9:

FROM ANGUISH TO HOPE

Ariella is part of a team of people who work with me. The team of physiotherapist, occupational therapist, speech therapist, case worker, social worker, care givers and my mom used to meet every few months to update their progress with me and create a future plan. Naturally, I was present and was invited to intervene or ask questions at any point. At the end of one of these meetings, Ariella noticed that I appeared agitated and upset. My facial expression was troubled. I became very quiet, shook my head a couple of times, and stared away from everyone out the window. Ariella could sense my rightful desire to be looked on as an equal, a person who had been interviewed on television for a talk show, a person who, despite my difficulties, is inspired to study, volunteer with those less fortunate, keep my slim figure by doing Pilates, swimming, disabled skiing and sailing, walking on the treadmill, and on the boardwalk. As she left, Ariella asked me to journal the experience and perhaps write a poem about it. In the poem I wrote, I expressed my feelings at that time.

Underestimated

UNDERESTIMATED
The feeling that nothing you do will be accepted as
HUMAN NATURE
After all you are not
NORMAL

Time to give up hope of ever being ACCEPTED
As normal
Everyone will tell you that as hard as you try you will always be
BRAIN INJURED

You cannot do anything productive on your own
In need of constant help from others
After all you are BRAIN INJURED
THE CURSE

It does not matter if you are talented at a task
You are obviously not doing it along
In need of help with every small task

The thought that you could have conquered this feat
On you own
RIDICULOUS

The thought of your being a responsible adult
Capable of the same feats as a NORMAL adult
Absolutely crazy
Sorry to have mentioned it

The thought of you despite your disability
Still striving for the same goal and feeling capable of conquering it
The people supporting you feeling they will give you a while
BEFORE REALITY HITS
Not understanding why you are
ANGRY

Where is this anger coming from?
Must be her
INJURY

NO! This is the explanation!!!!!

And day to day, I continue to live with my disability and try to focus on my ability. I try to reinvent myself.

Creation

Creating a personality from scratch
Trying to gather the frayed, torn pieces
Coming back to life and trying to rebuild it
Making sure that everything important to me before
Remains important
This has been the story of my new life.

Trying to make sure the same ideals still fit
Doing and trying new activities
To determine what the new me enjoys
Finding the limitations set on me by my new situation

In this world where the philosophy is
Survival of the fittest
The key to survival is
Not letting anyone tell me
What I am capable of

Given my new situation
Making sure I am the fittest possible
Facing and tackling each challenge
As if my life depended on it

This is the way a successful life is formed.

I continue with therapy, volunteer at schools and camps, go horseback riding, sail, ski, cycle, skydive, travel, study and socialize with family and friends. I still love nature and treasure the opportunities to write poetry. I express these enjoyable experiences in the following poems.

Peaceful time

Having hours to humbly relish and reflect
On the radiant and ravishing harbour
With the water washing away your worries
The bright beautiful sunshine breathtakingly
Beating down on the water
Warming the watchers on the walkway
Proud
Practising and producing poetry in the peaceful park

Is this illusionary?
Indeed

Time interrupted by immediate need to
Explore the environment
Time to transfer thoughts towards terminating terrible terrors

Solution?
Succumb to sensation and solve stressful situation
Decide to determine cause of stress and discover details
To make it disappear

The last poem in this book is an elegy to myself. In it I write about all the qualities I used to have before my accident, and in the last paragraph I list my new qualities. Surprisingly, though I face different challenges, I find my character remains the same. I also write about how I do my best to make myself appear efficient, calm and happy while keeping my stress inside.

A life lost?

An elegy to Jody Schloss, June 20, 1996

Fun to be with, easygoing, hard working, stubborn, determined,
steadfast, exciting, perfectionist and adventurous

Never afraid to try new things
Learn from experience

Consequences seem unfair
Deep sadness. A sought-after life wasted
The first anniversary, heart-breaking
Light a birthday candle
To celebrate an unwanted new beginning
A reminder of a wanted life forever vanished

A new beginning
A life full of challenges not faced before
Repeated "no's" and "not possible"
A stubborn girl remaining steadfast
Strong belief: No one can tell me what I am capable of
The challenge: to prove this to non-believers

Fun to be with, easygoing, hard working, stubborn, determined,
steadfast, exciting, perfectionist and adventurous
Never afraid to try new things
Learn from experience

A new life just beginning

AN INVITATION

So dear readers,

I tell my story. You retell it, with all of your own life experiences playing upon it, and suddenly it is your story. Then we tell our two stories to a third member of the story tribe, who listens to both and builds a new, personalized version that shocks us with its twists and turns, and causes us to re-cognize our self. And we are present at the birth of a new story; we now have three for our story bag, and every time [we] choose one of those stories to share, [we] will unknowingly, unwittingly include bits and scraps from all of them and suddenly I am telling a different story, but it is still mine, and the story is inside, outside and all around my head. Such is membership in the story culture. We tell our own stories – our daydreams, our gossip, our family anecdotes. We become human through our stories. (Booth & Barton, 2000, p.7)

Please read my story. Let it touch you. Reread it if you want to. Read it to a friend. Perhaps you will be inspired to write your own stories. Those that read stories want to write them.

REFERENCES:

Booth,D. & Barton, B. (2000). *Story Works.* Canada; Pembroke Publishers.

Leggo, C. (2004). Tangled lines: On autobiography and poetic knowing. In A.Cole, L. Neilsen, J.G. Knowles, T.C. Luciani (Eds.), *Provoked by art.* Canada; Backalong Books

O'Faolain, N. (2003). *Almost there.* New York, New York: Riverhead Books.

ACKNOWLEDGEMENTS

I started writing this book about 15 years ago when I had completely different goals, and was dealing with a lot of anger associated with my roll-over. When I finished writing this, I began the next chapter of my life after my accident. I went to Florida to train with a Paralympic athlete. I went to the Paralympics in 2012, and have been training in Florida every winter since then. Stay tuned for the Equestrian riding chapter or chapters of my life.

First and foremost I would like to thank Ariella Damelin for teaching me a very creative and positive way to release my emotions positively - through writing. A definite second who I don't think my recovery would be possible without is my loving parents and siblings. Especially my mom who drove every weekend to Erie, Pennsylvania to see me. Sometimes with her friend Paula (the Pom Pom lady) who blew loud horns on my birthday to let everyone in the hospital know that I was loved! Thank you to my many visitors in the hospital for making me feel so loved! My therapists there, and in Toronto during my initial recovery were amazing!

I went through many phases in my recovery in terms of finding out who I was, and finding out what and who I would become. Before my accident I loved working with children, and I always thought that I would be a teacher or therapist working with children with "special needs." Terms have changed, and the schooling system is much more inclusive now. I wanted to be a teacher for the deaf. I took up to level 3F in American Sign Language mostly at the Bob Rumball Centre for the Deaf. Thank you to Lori Dolomont Miller for teaching me so well! I continue to volunteer there now with a woman named Jackie; she really helped my comprehension! I also volunteered in the daycare, and loved it! Due to scientific advancements, Cochlear Implants replaced teaching ASL in the Deaf community, as such I would not be able to communicate effectively using ASL. My next step was to going to college to become an Educational Assistant. I worked in many schools and I learned a lot! Thank you especially to Jessica O'malley for helping me so much!

Before I started competing and riding professionally I was involved with sit-skiing in the winter months, and disabled sailing in the summer months. I loved both, and travelled all over Canada competing in sailing at the Mobility Cup, and all over North America sit-skiing. When I started competing at Para-Dressage internationally, I didn't have time to continue my other sports.

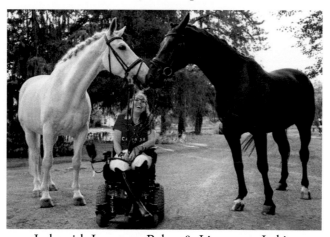

Jody with Inspector Rebus & Lieutenant Lobin

Printed in the United States
By Bookmasters